The Golden Years A Book - Questions an(from 1950s, 1960s, 1970s, 1980s - Music, TV, Movies, Sports and People

B N William

Copyright © 2024 by B N William

All rights reserved. No part of this book may be used or reproduced by any means, graphic, electronic, or mechanical, including photocopying, recording, taping, or by any information storage retrieval system, without the written permission of the publisher except in the case of brief quotations embodied in critical articles and reviews.

Contents

1950s	1
The Fabulous Fifties	1
Memory Lane	3
1950s	6
Answers for Trivia 1950s	17
1960s	41
The Swinging Sixties	41
Memory Lane	43
Quiz Time	45
Answers for Trivia 1960s	59
1970s	80
The Disco Decade	80
Memory Lane	82
1970s Cultural Highlights Disco Craze:	82
Answers for Trivia 1970s	92
1980s	116
The MTV Generation	116
Memory Lane	118
Quiz Time	120
Answers	140

1950s

The Fabulous Fifties

Story Time

Title: The Great TV Mix-Up of 1956

In the summer of 1956, in a small town in Iowa, the community was buzzing with excitement. Television was still a novelty, and the Johnson family had just gotten their very first set, a magnificent 21-inch screen encased in a polished wooden cabinet. It was the talk of the neighborhood, and Mr. Johnson proudly invited everyone over for a viewing party to watch the much-anticipated Elvis Presley appearance on "The Ed Sullivan Show."

The big night arrived, and the Johnson living room was packed with friends and neighbors. Mrs. Johnson had prepared her best snacks, and the air was filled with the smell of freshly popped popcorn. The excitement was palpable as everyone gathered around the television set, waiting for Elvis to grace the screen with his gyrating hips and soulful voice.

However, as the show started, the crowd's eager anticipation turned into puzzled murmurs. Instead of Elvis, the screen showed a documentary about penguins in Antarctica! Mr. Johnson fiddled with the dials and antennas, but no matter what he did, the penguins waddled on, seemingly indifferent to the disappointment they were causing in Iowa.

Little did the Johnsons know, they had gotten the date wrong – Elvis was scheduled for the following week. But as the evening went on, something magical happened. The group, initially dismayed, became fascinated by the penguin documentary. Laughter filled the room as they watched the comical antics of the birds, and soon they were all cheering for a particularly plucky penguin navigating its way through the icy landscape.

The evening ended up being a hit, and the Great TV Mix-Up of 1956 went down in local history. The following week, the Johnsons successfully hosted the Elvis viewing party, but many neighbors fondly remembered the penguin night as the best television experience they ever had. It was a gentle reminder that sometimes, joy comes from the most unexpected places.

Did you know that Elvis Presley was a black belt in karate and was awarded his black belt in 1960? He developed a deep passion for martial arts and incorporated karate moves into his stage performances, showcasing his dedication to both music and martial arts disciplines.

An interesting **lesser-known fact** about Elvis Presley is his passion for collecting police badges. From a young age, Elvis was fascinated by law enforcement and amassed a sizable collection of police badges from different departments across the United States. He even received honorary badges from several law enforcement agencies, showcasing his admiration for those who served in uniform.

Memory Lane

Rise of Rock 'n' Roll:

The 1950s witnessed the birth of rock 'n' roll, a revolutionary music genre. Elvis Presley's gyrating hips on stage, Chuck Berry's electrifying guitar riffs, and Little Richard's flamboyant performances were more than just entertainment; they were cultural milestones. Remember when "Tutti Frutti" first hit the airwaves, and teenagers across America couldn't help but dance along?

Iconic Movies:

The decade saw the silver screen dazzle with masterpieces. "Singin' in the Rain" brought joy with its unforgettable dance scenes. "Sunset Boulevard" captivated audiences with its dramatic tale, and "Rebel Without a Cause" became a symbol of youthful angst, introducing James Dean as a cultural icon. These films weren't just entertainment; they were a reflection of a changing society.

Television Boom:

Television transformed American homes, with shows like "I Love Lucy" bringing families together in laughter. "The Twilight Zone" took viewers on a journey into the unknown, while "Gunsmoke" captured the spirit of the Wild West. These shows weren't just pastimes; they shaped the American dream and became a nightly ritual for many.

Disneyland Opening:

In 1955, a magical world called Disneyland opened its gates in Anaheim, California. It was more than a theme park; it was a wonderland that turned fantasy into reality. Remember the awe and delight of watching Disneyland's first parade, with children's eyes lighting up at the sight of Mickey Mouse and Cinderella?

The Golden Age of Comics:

The '50s was a golden era for comic books, bringing superheroes like Superman and Batman into the limelight. These comics were more than just stories; they were escapes into worlds where good always triumphed over evil. Remember swapping comic books with friends and debating who

Sporting Triumph – The Miraculous Mile:

In May of 1954, a young medical student named Roger Bannister made history on a windy track in Oxford. Clocking a mile in under four minutes, Bannister shattered the belief that it was a feat beyond human capability. His "Miraculous Mile" was more than a record-breaking run; it was a triumph of the human spirit, proving that barriers were meant to be broken. Do you recall where you were when you heard the news? The excitement, the disbelief, and the overwhelming sense of pride? It was a moment when everyone felt they, too, could achieve the impossible.

Political Landmark – The Beginning of the Space Race:

The late 1950s ushered in an era of astronomical competition and ambition. With the Soviet Union launching Sputnik in 1957, the Space Race was ignited, becoming a pivotal chapter in the Cold War narrative. This wasn't just a satellite orbiting Earth; it was a demonstration of technological prowess and political might. The beep-beep sound of

Sputnik as it traversed the sky was not only a signal from space but a call to action, igniting a passion for space exploration across the

globe. Do you remember looking up at the night sky, wondering about the new frontier and dreaming of the possibilities it held?

Did you know that Chuck Berry, a pioneer of rock and roll music, was also a skilled pilot? In addition to his groundbreaking contributions to music, Berry obtained his pilot's license in the 1970s and often flew himself to his concert performances.

A **lesser-known fact** about Chuck Berry is that he had a brief but notable career in photography. In addition to his musical talents, Berry had a passion for capturing moments through the lens of a camera. He documented various aspects of his life and travels, providing a unique perspective into the world of one of rock and roll's most iconic figures.

Did you know that the launch of Sputnik also led to the creation of the International Geophysical Year (IGY) in 1957-1958, a collaborative scientific effort involving dozens of countries to study various aspects of the Earth and space?

Did you know that in the 1950s, Oxford University made significant strides in scientific research, including the development of the first commercial nuclear power station

A **lesser-known fact** about Gunsmoke: During its run on television, the show faced cancellation after its first season due to low ratings. However, CBS decided to renew it at the last minute after receiving an overwhelming number of letters from fans who loved the show.

1950s

Which classic TV show featured the characters Lucy and Ricky Ricardo?

- The Twilight Zone
- I Love Lucy
- Gunsmoke

Who wrote the novel 'Fahrenheit 451,' which was published in the 1950s?

- George Orwell
- Aldous Huxley
- Ray Bradbury

In 1959, which film won the Academy Award for Best Picture?

- Ben-Hur
- Some Like It Hot
- North by Northwest

Which actress starred in the Alfred Hitchcock classic 'Rear Window'?

- Audrey Hepburn
- Grace Kelly
- Marilyn Monroe

Question: Which actress starred in the Alfred Hitchcock classic 'Rear Window'?

What was Elvis Presley's first hit in 1956?

- Jailhouse Rock
- Love Me Tender
- Heartbreak Hotel Answer

Which television game show made its debut in 1956 and is still running today?

- The Price is Right
- What's My Line?
- To Tell the Truth

Did you know that the first televised game show in the United States was "Truth or Consequences," which debuted in 1941?

Who starred as the lead role in the 1953 film 'Roman Holiday'?

- Audrey Hepburn
- Elizabeth Taylor
- Katharine Hepburn

Which famous music group was formed in Liverpool in the late 1950s?

- The Beatles
- The Rolling Stones
- The Beach Boys

What was the name of the first-ever animated feature film produced by Walt Disney in the 1950s?

- Sleeping Beauty
- Cinderella
- Snow White and the Seven Dwarfs

Did you know that Walt Disney, the founder of The Walt Disney Company, was afraid of mice? This fear inspired him to create one of the most iconic cartoon characters of all time: Mickey Mouse.

Which iconic 1950s movie featured the song 'As Time Goes By'?

- Singin' in the
- Rain Casablanca
- An American in Paris

1950s Trivia Questions: Historical Milestones

What significant political event occurred in Germany in 1953?

- The Berlin Wall was built.
- The Berlin Airlift ended.
- The Uprising in East Berlin.

Who became the leader of the Soviet Union after Stalin's death in 1953?

- Nikita Khrushchev
- Leonid Brezhnev
- Georgy Malenkov

Did you know that Joseph Stalin, the leader of the Soviet Union, had a peculiar fondness for American Western films? Despite his iron-fisted rule, he couldn't resist the allure of cowboy adventures from Hollywood!

In 1954, the Supreme Court made a landmark decision in which case?

- Brown v. Board of Education
- Roe v. Wade
- Miranda v. Arizona

Which country gained independence from France in 1954?

- Vietnam
- Algeria
- Morocco

In 1957, which country launched the first artificial satellite?

- United States
- Soviet Union
- United Kingdom

Did you know that the Soviet Union's secret police, the KGB, once used hollowed-out copies of "The Gulag Archipelago" by Aleksandr Solzhenitsyn to smuggle banned Western literature into the country?

What was the major development in the United States' Civil Rights Movement in 1955?

- The Montgomery Bus Boycott
- The founding of the Black Panther Party
- The March on Washington

Which Asian country was admitted to the United Nations in 1955?

- Japan
- China
- India

What historic event happened in Antarctica in 1959?

- The Antarctic Treaty was signed.
- The first human reached the South Pole.
- Discovery of underwater lakes.

Did you know that the United Nations once held a "World Happiness Report," ranking countries based on factors like income, social support, and life expectancy?

In 1958, NASA was established in response to what event?

- The Apollo 1 disaster.
- The launch of Sputnik.
- The first moon landing.

Who was elected as the Prime Minister of the United Kingdom in 1955?

- Winston Churchill
- Anthony Eden
- Harold Macmillan

Which fashion trend, characterized by a full skirt and a cinched waistline, was popular among women in the 1950s?

- The Pencil Skirt
- The A-Line Dress
- The Circle Skirt

Did you know that Winston Churchill, the iconic British Prime Minister, was an accomplished painter who produced over 500 works of art during his lifetime?

Which type of jacket, often associated with James Dean and Marlon Brando, became a symbol of teen rebellion in the 1950s?

- The Denim Jacket
- The Bomber Jacket
- The Leather Jacket ✓

What was the popular hairstyle for men, characterized by slicked-back hair, in the 1950s?

- The Crew Cut
- The Pompadour
- The Mullet

In interior design, which item became a must-have in every 1950s living room?

- The Chaise Lounge
- The Television Set ✓
- The Rocking Chair

Did you know that James Dean was a skilled car racer who competed in several professional races during his short life? His passion for racing paralleled his rebellious persona on-screen.

What footwear became popular among teenagers in the 1950s, especially with the advent of rock 'n' roll?

- Loafers
- Saddle Shoes
- High Heels

Which iconic toy, first introduced in the late 1950s, became a household name for children?

- Barbie Doll
- G.I. Joe
- Lego Bricks

What type of eyewear became trendy in the 1950s, especially among women?

- Aviator Sunglasses
- Cat-Eye Glasses
- Round Spectacles

Did you know that G.I. Joe, the iconic action figure, was inducted into the National Toy Hall of Fame in 2004 for its significant cultural impact and enduring popularity?

Which 1950s innovation in home appliances made food preparation easier and quicker?

- The Electric Mixer
- The Microwave Oven
- The Dishwasher

What was the first commercially available vaccine developed by Jonas Salk in the 1950s?

- Measles
- Polio
- Tuberculosis

Which device, vital for heart surgery, was invented by John Gibbon in 1953?

- The Pacemaker
- The Heart-Lung Machine
- The Stethoscope

Did you know that in the 1950s, Ghana became the first African country to gain independence from colonial rule, inspiring nationalist movements across the continent and paving the way for decolonization?

In 1957, the first portable transistor radio, the TR-63, was released by which company?

- Sony
- RCA
- Philips

Which color television system became the standard in the United States in the 1950s?

- NTSC
- PAL
- SECAM

Which antibiotic, still widely used today, was first introduced in the 1950s?

- Penicillin
- Tetracycline
- Erythromycin

Did you know that the first publicly demonstrated color television system was developed by John Logie Baird in 1928, years before commercially successful color television systems became available?

What type of nuclear power reactor was commissioned for the first time in 1954?

- Pressurized Water Reactor
- Boiling Water Reactor
- Sodium-cooled Fast Reactor Answer:

The first commercial videotape recorder was released in 1956 by which company?

- Sony
- Ampex
- Panasonic Ampex

Who won the World Cup in soccer in 1950?

- Brazil
- Uruguay
- Italy

Did you know that the FIFA World Cup, the most prestigious international soccer tournament, was first held in 1930 and has since grown to become the most widely viewed sporting event in the world, even surpassing the Olympics in terms of global viewership?

Which athlete broke the color barrier in Major League Baseball in 1947 and continued to impact the sport throughout the 1950s?

- Willie Mays
- Hank Aaron
- Jackie Robinson

In 1954, Roger Bannister became the first person to run a mile in under how many minutes?

- Four minutes
- Three and a half minutes
- Five minutes

Which famous golfer won his first Masters Tournament in 1958?

- Arnold Palmer
- Jack Nicklaus
- Gary Player

Did you know that Major League Baseball (MLB) has been played since 1869 and is the oldest professional sports league in the United States?

In which year did the Boston Celtics win their first NBA Championship, marking the start of a dynasty?

- A) 1957
- B) 1959
- C) 1955

Who set the world record in the 100m dash in 1956 and was known as the 'World's Fastest Human'?

- Jesse Owens
- Bob Hayes
- Wilma Rudolph

Who won the Wimbledon Men's Singles title five times throughout the 1950s?

- Rod Laver
- Bjorn Borg
- Lew Hoad

Did you know that Wimbledon, the oldest tennis tournament in the world, has been held since 1877 and is renowned for its traditions, like the strict dress code of predominantly white attire?

Which team won the first-ever NFL Championship game televised nationally in the United S

- Cleveland Browns
- Los Angeles Rams
- New York Giants

The first Pan American Games were held in 1951 in which city?

- Buenos Aires, Argentina
- Mexico City, Mexico
- Havana, Cuba

Did you know that Havana, the capital city of Cuba, is home to the world's largest collection of colonial-era architecture in the Americas? Its historic center, Old Havana, is a UNESCO World Heritage Site and showcases stunning examples of Spanish colonial architecture, colorful buildings, and cobblestone streets.

Answers for Trivia 1950s

Question: Which classic TV show featured the characters Lucy and Ricky Ricardo?

Answer: I Love Lucy

Trivia Snapshot: "I Love Lucy," starring Lucille Ball and Desi Arnaz, premiered in 1951 and quickly became one of the most beloved shows in American television history. The show was groundbreaking in many ways, including its portrayal of an interracial marriage between Lucy Ricardo and Ricky Ricardo, a Cuban bandleader. Lucille Ball's comedic genius and the show's innovative use of a live studio audience and a three-camera setup revolutionized TV production. "I Love Lucy" also introduced the rerun, which allowed it to gain new audiences over the decades and remain a staple of TV syndication.

Question: Who wrote the novel 'Fahrenheit 451,' which was published in the 1950s?

Answer: Ray Bradbury

Trivia Snapshot: Ray Bradbury's 'Fahrenheit 451,' published in 1953, is a dystopian novel set in a future where books are banned and "firemen" burn any that are found. The title refers to the temperature at which book paper catches fire and burns. The novel is a critique of censorship and a warning against the passive consumption of broadcast media. Bradbury, who was concerned about the rise of television and the decline of literature, expressed his fears that television would kill interest in reading books, a theme deeply embedded in the narrative of 'Fahrenheit 451.' The novel remains a staple in discussions about censorship, freedom of expression, and the role of literature in society.

Question: In 1959, which film won the Academy Award for Best Picture?

Answer: Ben-Hur ✗

Trivia Snapshot: 'Ben-Hur,' directed by William Wyler, is known for its epic scale, including the famous chariot race scene, which remains one of cinema's most celebrated sequences. The film set a record at the time by winning eleven Academy Awards, a feat equaled only by 'Titanic' and 'The Lord of the Rings: The Return of the King' in later years. The immense set, thousands of extras, and groundbreaking special effects made 'Ben-Hur' a monumental achievement in film history.

Question: Which actress starred in the Alfred Hitchcock classic 'Rear Window'?

Answer: Grace Kelly ✓

Trivia Snapshot: Grace Kelly's performance in 'Rear Window' (1954), alongside James Stewart, is one of her most memorable roles. Directed by Alfred Hitchcock, the film is a masterful suspense thriller that takes place almost entirely in a single room. Kelly's elegance and charm, coupled with Hitchcock's direction, create a tense and engaging narrative. Her film career was short-lived, as she retired from acting at the age of 26 to marry Prince Rainier III of Monaco.

Question: What was Elvis Presley's first hit in 1956?

Answer: Heartbreak Hotel ✗

Trivia Snapshot: "Heartbreak Hotel" became Elvis Presley's first No. 1 hit on the Billboard music charts and is often regarded as the song that established his career as a rock 'n' roll icon.

Released in January 1956, the song was inspired by a newspaper article about a man who jumped to his death from a hotel window, leaving behind a note with the line, "I walk a lonely street." The song's success was meteoric, staying at the top of the charts for seven weeks, and it marked the beginning of Presley's ascent to international stardom.

Question: Which television game show made its debut in 1956 and is still running today?

Answer: The Price is Right

Trivia Snapshot: 'The Price is Right,' first hosted by Bill Cullen, debuted in 1956 and has become one of the longest- running game shows in television history. It gained immense popularity for its unique format of contestants guessing the prices of merchandise to win cash and prizes. Bob Barker became synonymous with the show from 1972 to 2007, followed

by Drew Carey. Its longevity and adaptability have made it a staple of American daytime television, capturing the hearts of multiple generations.

Question: Who starred as the lead role in the 1953 film 'Roman Holiday'?

Answer: Audrey Hepburn

Trivia Snapshot: Audrey Hepburn's performance in 'Roman Holiday' marked her first major role and led to her winning the Academy Award for Best Actress. Hepburn's portrayal of a royal princess exploring Rome incognito captured the hearts of audiences worldwide. The film, also starring Gregory Peck, became an instant classic, showcasing Hepburn's charm and talent and establishing her as one of Hollywood's greatest actresses.

Question: Which famous music group was formed in Liverpool in the late 1950s?

Answer: The Beatles ✓

Trivia Snapshot: The Beatles, formed in Liverpool in 1960, revolutionized the music industry and became a defining symbol of the '60s counterculture. Originally consisting of John Lennon, Paul McCartney, George Harrison, and Ringo Starr, the band achieved unprecedented popularity and critical acclaim. Their innovative songwriting and style of music had a significant impact on the culture and music of the era, leading them to be regarded as one of the greatest and most influential bands in history.

Question: What was the name of the first-ever animated feature film produced by Walt Disney in the 1950s?

Answer: Cinderella ✗

Trivia Snapshot: "Cinderella," released in 1950, marked Disney's return to feature-length animated films after World War II. The film's success played a crucial role in revitalizing the Walt Disney Company. Based on the classic fairy tale, "Cinderella" became one of Disney's most iconic and enduring films, known for its memorable music and timeless story. It helped cement Disney's reputation as the leading creator of animated fairy tales.

Question: Which iconic 1950s movie featured the song 'As Time Goes By'?

Answer: Casablanca

Trivia Snapshot: "Casablanca," though released in 1942, remained a quintessential film of the 1950s and beyond. The song "As Time Goes By," performed by Dooley Wilson in the movie, became intrinsically linked to the film's romantic and nostalgic essence. Set against the backdrop of World War II, "Casablanca" is celebrated for its timeless story of love and sacrifice, with Humphrey Bogart and Ingrid Bergman's performances becoming iconic in film history.

Question: What significant political event occurred in Germany in 1953?

Answer: The Uprising in East Berlin

Trivia Snapshot: The Uprising in East Berlin on June 17, 1953, was a significant event during the Cold War. It was a workers' revolt against the government of the German Democratic Republic (GDR) and spread throughout East Germany. The uprising was a response to rising work quotas and poor living conditions. Despite being violently suppressed by Soviet armed forces, it was an early sign of resistance against the Communist government in East Germany and highlighted the growing discontent among its citizens. The date, June 17, was later observed in West Germany as a day in memory of the struggle for freedom in East Germany.

Question: Who became the leader of the Soviet Union after Stalin's death in 1953?

Answer: Nikita Khrushchev

Trivia Snapshot: Nikita Khrushchev emerged as the leader of the Soviet Union after Joseph Stalin's death in 1953. He became First Secretary of the Communist Party and later Premier of the Soviet Union. Khrushchev is best remembered for initiating the "De-Stalinization" process, which sought to reduce the use of terror and soften the authoritarian control

of the regime. He famously criticized Stalin's rule in his "Secret Speech" in 1956, leading to significant changes in the Soviet Union and impacting the international communist movement.

Question: In 1954, the Supreme Court made a landmark decision in which case?

Answer: Brown v. Board of Education

Trivia Snapshot: The Supreme Court's decision in "Brown v. Board of Education" in 1954 was a monumental moment in the Civil Rights Movement. This landmark case declared state laws establishing separate public schools for black and white students to be unconstitutional, effectively overturning the "separate but equal" doctrine established by the Plessy v.

Ferguson decision in 1896. The ruling was a major victory for the NAACP and a pivotal step towards desegregation, setting the stage for further civil rights advancements in the United States.

Question: Which country gained independence from France in 1954?

Answer: Vietnam

Trivia Snapshot: Vietnam gained its independence from France in 1954 following the decisive Battle of Dien Bien Phu. This marked the end of the First Indochina War and led to the Geneva Accords, which temporarily separated Vietnam at the 17th parallel into North Vietnam and South Vietnam. This division set the stage for the Vietnam War, a major conflict that further shaped the country's history and had significant global implications during the Cold War era.

Question: In 1957, which country launched the first artificial satellite?

Answer: Soviet Union

Trivia Snapshot: The Soviet Union made a historic achievement in space exploration by launching the first artificial satellite, Sputnik 1, on October 4, 1957. This event marked the start of the space age and the U.S.-Soviet space race. Sputnik's launch proved that human-made objects could orbit the Earth, a significant milestone in human history. The satellite's beeping signals were heard by radio operators around the world, symbolizing the dawn of a new era in technology and exploration.

Question: What was the major development in the United States' Civil Rights Movement in 1955?

Answer: The Montgomery Bus Boycott ✓

Trivia Snapshot: The Montgomery Bus Boycott, initiated in 1955, was a pivotal event in the American Civil Rights Movement. Sparked by Rosa Parks' refusal to give up her seat to a white passenger, the boycott lasted over a year and led to a Supreme Court ruling that declared segregation on public buses unconstitutional. This nonviolent protest, involving the African American community of Montgomery, Alabama, catapulted Martin Luther King Jr. to national prominence as a civil rights leader and set the stage for future civil rights activism in the United States.

Question: Which Asian country was admitted to the United Nations in 1955?

Answer: Japan

Trivia Snapshot: Japan's admission to the United Nations in 1955 marked a significant milestone in the country's post- World War II rehabilitation and reintegration into the international community. This event symbolized Japan's transition from a militaristic past to a peaceful, democratic nation committed to global cooperation. Japan's entry into the UN was a key step in re-establishing its sovereignty and beginning its rise as a significant global economic power.

Question: What historic event happened in Antarctica in 1959?

Answer: A) The Antarctic Treaty was signed

Trivia Snapshot: The signing of the Antarctic Treaty in 1959 represented a landmark achievement in international diplomacy and cooperation. The treaty, originally signed by 12 countries, set aside Antarctica as a scientific preserve, established freedom of scientific investigation, and banned military activity on the continent. This agreement was pivotal in ensuring that Antarctica remained a place for peaceful research and exploration, free from the geopolitical tensions of the Cold War era.

Question: In 1958, NASA was established in response to what event?

Answer: The launch of Sputnik

Trivia Snapshot: The establishment of NASA (National Aeronautics and Space Administration) in 1958 was a direct response to the Soviet Union's launch of Sputnik, the world's first artificial satellite, in 1957. Sputnik's launch marked the beginning of the space race and prompted the United States to prioritize space exploration and technology. NASA's creation signaled a significant commitment by the U.S. government to not only compete in space exploration but also to foster scientific advancements and aeronautic research.

Question: Who was elected as the Prime Minister of the United Kingdom in 1955?

Answer: Anthony Eden

Trivia Snapshot: Anthony Eden succeeded Winston Churchill as the Prime Minister of the United Kingdom in 1955. Eden had a long career in British politics, having previously served as Foreign Secretary. His term as Prime Minister, however, was overshadowed by the Suez Crisis of 1956, a major international incident that diminished Britain's influence on the world stage and

ultimately led to Eden's resignation in 1957. The Suez Crisis was a defining moment in post-war British history, symbolizing the end of Britain's role as a major world power.

Question: Which fashion trend, characterized by a full skirt and a cinched waistline, was popular among women in the 1950s?

Answer: The Circle Skirt

Trivia Snapshot: The circle skirt became a fashion sensation in the 1950s, epitomizing the era's feminine style. Its full, flared design, often accentuated with petticoats, and cinched waist created a silhouette that was both playful and elegant. This style was popularized by designers like Christian Dior and became synonymous with 50s fashion. The circle skirt reflected the post- war optimism and the era's emphasis on youth and vibrancy, making it a staple in the wardrobe of the modern 1950s woman.

Question: Which type of jacket, often associated with James Dean and Marlon Brando, became a symbol of teen rebellion in the 1950s?

Answer: The Leather Jacket

Trivia Snapshot: The leather jacket became an iconic symbol of youth rebellion in the 1950s, largely due to its association with Hollywood stars like James Dean and Marlon Brando. Brando's appearance in the 1953 film "The Wild One" particularly popularized the leather jacket, making it a staple of the rebellious teen's wardrobe. The jacket's rugged and durable nature, along with its association with motorcycle culture, embodied the spirit of rebellion and nonconformity that defined the youth culture of the 50s.

Question: What was the popular hairstyle for men, characterized by slicked-back hair, in the 1950s?

Answer: The Pompadour

Trivia Snapshot: The Pompadour hairstyle, characterized by hair swept upwards from the face and worn high over the forehead, became popular among men in the 1950s. It was famously sported by cultural icons like Elvis Presley, adding to its appeal among the youth. The style was a sign of the flamboyant and rebellious spirit of the times, deviating from the more conservative hairstyles of previous decades. The Pompadour remains a classic hairstyle, symbolizing the blend of elegance and edginess that defined 50s fashion.

Question: In interior design, which item became a must-have in every 1950s living room?

Answer: The Television Set

Trivia Snapshot: The 1950s saw the television set become an essential part of home life in America and many parts of the world. As TV programming expanded, the television quickly turned from a luxury item into a must-have household appliance, significantly changing family life and entertainment. Popular shows like "I Love Lucy" and "The Ed Sullivan Show" became common conversation topics, and the TV set itself became a focal point in living room designs. The rise of television marked a shift in culture and society, paving the way for the mass media's influence in the latter half of the 20th century.

Question: What footwear became popular among teenagers in the 1950s, especially with the advent of rock 'n' roll?

Answer: Saddle Shoes

Trivia Snapshot: Saddle shoes, characterized by their distinctive two-tone leather construction, became a fashion staple for American teenagers in the 1950s, particularly with the rise of rock 'n' roll music. Often worn with bobby socks by girls, these shoes were associated with the clean-cut, all-American style that was prevalent during the era. The popularity of saddle shoes was also boosted by their appearance in movies and on television shows that depicted the idealized suburban lifestyle of the 50s.

Question: Which iconic toy, first introduced in the late 1950s, became a household name for children?

Answer: Barbie Doll ✓

Trivia Snapshot: The Barbie doll, introduced by American toy company Mattel in 1959, quickly became a cultural icon and one of the most popular toys of the 20th century. Created by Ruth Handler and named after her daughter, Barbara, Barbie was one of the first mass-produced toys to focus on adult-like figures rather than infants. The doll was revolutionary in the way it represented a new role model for girls, allowing them to imagine themselves in adult roles and careers. Barbie's vast wardrobe and various incarnations also made her a significant figure in children's fashion play.

Question: What type of eyewear became trendy in the 1950s, especially among women?

Answer: Cat-Eye Glasses ✓

Trivia Snapshot: Cat-eye glasses, known for their upswept angles and rounded frames, became a fashion trend among women in the 1950s. They were a part of the larger feminine aesthetic of the era, often embellished with rhinestones and intricate designs. Celebrities like Marilyn

Monroe and Audrey Hepburn popularized these glasses, making them a symbol of glamour and sophistication. The cat-eye style reflected the era's emphasis on bold, dramatic fashion statements and continues to be revisited in modern fashion trends.

Question: Which 1950s innovation in home appliances made food preparation easier and quicker?

Answer: The Microwave Oven ✓

Trivia Snapshot: The microwave oven, first introduced to the consumer market in the 1950s, revolutionized home cooking by drastically reducing the time needed to heat food. Initially, microwave ovens were quite large and expensive, making them less accessible to the average household. However, as the technology improved and prices dropped, they became a common appliance in most homes. The microwave oven's invention is attributed to Percy Spencer, who discovered microwave heating by accident while working with radar technology during World War II.

Question: In the 1950s, what trend emerged in teenage culture, characterized by listening to rock 'n' roll music and wearing casual, rebellious clothing?

Answer: Greaser

Trivia Snapshot: The 'Greaser' subculture emerged in the 1950s among American teenagers, influenced heavily by rock 'n' roll music and films like "Rebel Without a Cause." Greasers were known for their distinctive style, including leather jackets, jeans, slicked-back hair, and an overall rebellious attitude. This subculture was seen as a form of resistance against the mainstream, conservative norms of the era and was often associated with the working-class youth. The Greaser style and attitude had a significant impact on fashion and youth culture, leaving a

lasting legacy in American pop culture.

Question: Which popular dance style, often seen on American Bandstand, became a craze among teens in the late 1950s?

Answer: The Jitterbug

Trivia Snapshot: The Jitterbug, a lively dance style that emerged in the 1930s and gained widespread popularity in the 1950s, became synonymous with the youth culture of the era. It was often featured on shows like "American Bandstand," where teenagers showcased their energetic dance moves. The Jitterbug included a variety of styles, such as the Lindy Hop and swing, and was known for its acrobatic and improvisational nature. The dance was a reflection of the exuberant spirit of the post-war era and has remained a significant part of American dance history. Question: What was the first commercially available vaccine developed by Jonas Salk in the 1950s?

Answer: Polio

Trivia Snapshot: Jonas Salk's development of the polio vaccine in the 1950s was a monumental achievement in medical science. Introduced in 1955, the vaccine effectively tackled the poliovirus, which had caused widespread fear due to its crippling effects, particularly on children. The vaccine's success led to a dramatic decrease in polio cases worldwide and paved the way for the eventual eradication of the disease in many countries. Salk's refusal to patent the vaccine, ensuring it would be widely accessible, further solidified his legacy as a champion of public health.

Question: Which device, vital for heart surgery, was invented by John Gibbon in 1953?

Answer: The Heart-Lung Machine

Trivia Snapshot: The invention of the heart-lung machine by Dr. John Gibbon in 1953 marked a significant advancement in cardiac surgery. This machine temporarily takes over the function of the heart and lungs during surgery, allowing surgeons to operate on a still heart. The development of this technology made complex procedures like open-heart surgery possible, saving countless lives. Gibbon's invention was a milestone in medical history, revolutionizing cardiac care and treatment.

Question: In 1957, the first portable transistor radio, the TR-63, was released by which company?

Answer: Sony

Trivia Snapshot: Sony's release of the TR-63 transistor radio in 1957 marked a significant advancement in consumer electronics. The TR-63 was the world's first truly pocket-sized transistor radio and its portability transformed the way people listened to music and news, making it possible to enjoy radio broadcasts from anywhere. This innovation not only popularized transistor radios but also established Sony as a major player in the electronics industry, paving the way for the company's future successes in various fields of technology.

Question: Which color television system became the standard in the United States in the 1950s?

Answer: NTSC

Trivia Snapshot: NTSC (National Television System Committee) became the standard color television system in the United States in the 1950s. Developed in 1953, NTSC was the first widely adopted standard for color TV broadcasting and played a crucial role in the transition from black and white to color television. The adoption of the NTSC standard marked a new era in television history, significantly enhancing the viewing experience and paving the way for the future of broadcast television.

Question: What significant medical breakthrough occurred in 1953 in the field of genetics?

Answer: Discovery of the DNA double helix structure

Trivia Snapshot: The discovery of the DNA double helix structure in 1953 by James Watson and Francis Crick was a groundbreaking moment in the field of genetics. Their work, building on the research of Rosalind Franklin and Maurice Wilkins, revealed the double helix shape of the DNA molecule, providing fundamental insight into the genetic code and mechanisms of heredity. This discovery revolutionized biology and medicine, leading to numerous scientific and medical advances, including the Human Genome Project.

Question: Who invented the first practical solar cell in 1954?

Answer: Bell Labs

Trivia Snapshot: The invention of the first practical solar cell by Bell Labs in 1954 marked the beginning of modern solar energy technology. This solar cell was capable of converting sunlight into electrical energy with an efficiency of about 6%, a significant achievement at the time. The development of this technology laid the foundation for the use of solar power as a renewable energy source, opening up new possibilities for sustainable and clean energy. Bell Labs' innovation was a crucial step in the evolution of solar energy systems that are widely used today.

Question: What was launched into space in 1957, becoming the world's first artificial satellite?

Answer: Sputnik I

Trivia Snapshot: Sputnik I, launched by the Soviet Union on October 4, 1957, marked the beginning of the space age and the start of the space race between the United States and the Soviet Union. As the world's first artificial satellite, Sputnik's successful launch into orbit was a significant achievement in space exploration and a moment of great scientific advancement. Its launch demonstrated the feasibility of sending objects into orbit and led to the development of more advanced satellites and space exploration missions, including human spaceflight.

Question: Which antibiotic, still widely used today, was first introduced in the 1950s?

Answer: Tetracycline

Trivia Snapshot: Tetracycline, introduced in the early 1950s, became one of the most widely used antibiotics for its effectiveness against a broad range of bacterial infections. The development of tetracycline represented a major advancement in antibiotic therapy. Its ability to treat various infectious diseases, including pneumonia, acne, and chlamydia, made it a significant tool in medical treatment. Tetracycline's impact is notable in its ongoing use in modern medicine, despite the emergence of antibiotic resistance over the years.

Question: What type of nuclear power reactor was commissioned for the first time in 1954?

Answer: Pressurized Water Reactor

Trivia Snapshot: The world's first pressurized water reactor (PWR) for nuclear power, the USS Nautilus submarine's reactor, was commissioned in 1954. This event marked a significant milestone in the peaceful use of nuclear energy. The PWR design, in which water is heated under high pressure to prevent boiling, became a popular choice for civilian nuclear power generation. The technology's development for the Nautilus paved the way for the widespread adoption of nuclear power as a major source of electricity, revolutionizing the energy sector.

Question: The first commercial videotape recorder was released in 1956 by which company?

Answer: Ampex

Trivia Snapshot: Ampex, an American electronics company, released the first commercially successful videotape recorder (VTR) in 1956. This innovation revolutionized the television industry by allowing programs to be recorded and broadcast with greater flexibility and quality.

Before the advent of the VTR, television programs were broadcast live or recorded on

kinescope film, which was of lower quality. The introduction of the videotape recorder by Ampex significantly enhanced the production and distribution of television content, changing the industry forever.

Question: Who won the World Cup in soccer in 1950?

Answer: Uruguay

Trivia Snapshot: Uruguay's victory in the 1950 FIFA World Cup, held in Brazil, was a historic moment in the world of soccer. Their win in the final against Brazil, in a match often referred to as the "Maracanazo," is considered one of the biggest upsets in World Cup history. Played in front of a record-breaking crowd at the Maracanã Stadium in Rio de

Janeiro, Uruguay's win was their second World Cup triumph, following their inaugural victory in 1930. This match left a lasting legacy in the soccer world and is remembered as a classic example of the unpredictable nature of the sport.

Question: Which athlete broke the color barrier in Major League Baseball in 1947 and continued to impact the sport throughout the 1950s?

Answer: Jackie Robinson

Trivia Snapshot: Jackie Robinson's debut with the Brooklyn Dodgers in 1947 made him the first African American to play in Major League Baseball in the modern era, breaking the baseball color line. His entry into the league was a significant moment in both sports history and the American Civil Rights Movement. Robinson faced considerable racial discrimination and hostility but became a powerful symbol of integration and change. His on-field success and off-field dignity helped pave the way for further integration in sports.

Question: In 1954, Roger Bannister became the first person to run a mile in under how many minutes?

Answer: Four minutes

Trivia Snapshot: On May 6, 1954, British athlete Roger Bannister made history by running the first sub-four-minute mile at a track meet in Oxford, England. His record time of 3 minutes 59.4 seconds broke a psychological barrier, proving that it was possible to run a mile in under four minutes. This historic achievement was a landmark moment in the world of athletics and is still celebrated as a symbol of human endurance and potential.

Question: Which famous golfer won his first Masters Tournament in 1958?

Answer: Arnold Palmer

Trivia Snapshot: Arnold Palmer's victory in the 1958 Masters Tournament marked the beginning of his legendary career in golf. This win at Augusta National Golf Club was the first of his four Masters victories. Palmer, known for his charismatic personality and aggressive style of play, became one of golf's most popular and influential figures. His success helped to popularize and bring the sport of golf to a broader audience. Palmer's contributions to the game extended beyond his playing career, including his involvement in golf course design and the creation of the PGA Tour.

Question: In which year did the Boston Celtics win their first NBA Championship, marking the start of a dynasty?

Answer: 1957

Trivia Snapshot: The Boston Celtics' first NBA Championship victory in 1957 marked the beginning of one of the most dominant dynasties in sports history. Under the leadership of coach Red Auerbach and with key players like Bill Russell, the Celtics defeated the St. Louis

Hawks to claim the title. This victory was the first of 17 championships for the Celtics, establishing them as a powerhouse in the NBA. The Celtics' dominance in the late 1950s and throughout the 1960s set a high standard for excellence and team play in professional basketball.

Question: Who set the world record in the 100m dash in 1956 and was known as the 'World's Fastest Human'?

Answer: Bob Hayes

Trivia Snapshot: Bob Hayes, known as "Bullet Bob" for his incredible speed, set numerous world records in sprinting. Although he set significant records in the 1960s, his achievements in the 100m dash made him a standout athlete of his time. Hayes' remarkable speed later led him to a successful career in professional football, where he continued to demonstrate his athletic prowess as a wide receiver. His dual-sport success has made him one of the most celebrated athletes in track and field and football history.

Question: Which boxer was the world heavyweight champion from 1952 to 1956?

Answer: Rocky Marciano

Trivia Snapshot: Rocky Marciano is celebrated as one of the greatest heavyweight boxers of all time. Holding the world heavyweight title from 1952 to 1956, he retired undefeated, a feat unmatched by any other heavyweight champion. With a record of 49 wins, including 43 knockouts, Marciano was known for his power, endurance, and relentless fighting style. His remarkable career and undefeated record have left an indelible mark on the world of boxing, making him a symbol of strength and perseverance in the sport.

Question: Who won the Wimbledon Men's Singles title five times throughout the 1950s?

Answer: Lew Hoad

Trivia Snapshot: Lew Hoad, an Australian tennis player, was one of the dominant forces in tennis during the 1950s. However, contrary to the provided answer, Hoad won the Wimbledon Men's Singles title twice, in 1956 and 1957. He was renowned for his powerful serve and volley game, athleticism, and competitive spirit. Hoad's rivalry with fellow Australian Ken Rosewall is legendary in tennis history. His achievements in the 1950s, including multiple Grand Slam titles, have secured his place as one of the greats of the sport.

Question: Which team won the first-ever NFL Championship game televised nationally in the United States in 1951?

Answer: Los Angeles Rams

Trivia Snapshot: The Los Angeles Rams won the NFL Championship in 1951, marking their first championship victory since the team moved to Los Angeles. The championship game, played against the Cleveland Browns, was significant as it was the first NFL Championship to be televised nationally in the United States. This game was a turning point in the history of the NFL, showcasing the growing popularity of American football and setting the stage for the sport's future success on television.

Question: The first Pan American Games were held in 1951 in which city?

Answer: Buenos Aires, Argentina

Trivia Snapshot: The first Pan American Games, held in Buenos Aires, Argentina, in 1951, were a major step in the development of sports in the Americas. The games brought together athletes from across the Western Hemisphere to compete in various sports, similar to the Olympics. This event was crucial for fostering athletic talent and sportsmanship in the Americas and has since become an important fixture in the international sports calendar, held every four years. The Pan American Games have played a significant role in promoting unity and cultural exchange among the nations of the Americas

Did you know that Buenos Aires, the capital of Argentina, is often called the "Paris of South America" due to its European-inspired architecture, wide boulevards, and rich cultural heritage? It's a city known for its passionate tango dancing, delicious cuisine, and vibrant arts scene, making it a captivating destination for travelers from around the world.

Did you know that Los Angeles was once the site of one of the largest oil fields in the United States? The discovery of oil in the late 19th century transformed the city into a major oil-producing region, fueling its rapid growth and economic development.

Did you know that the Boston Celtics basketball team derived their name from Boston's significant Irish population and the city's historic connection to Celtic culture, particularly the Irish immigrants who settled in the area? This connection pays homage to Ireland's rich heritage and adds a cultural dimension to the team's identity.

Did you know that the PGA Tour, one of the premier professional golf circuits in the world, was originally formed by a group of professional golfers who sought to standardize tournament rules and create a more organized schedule of events? Established in 1929, the PGA Tour has since grown into a global phenomenon, showcasing the talents of the world's top golfers and captivating audiences worldwide.

1960s

The Swinging Sixties

1960s

Story Time

The Day the Beatles Came to Maplewood

It was the summer of 1964, and the small town of Maplewood was buzzing with an unusual energy. The Beatles, the biggest band in the world, were on their first American tour, and due to a quirky twist of fate, they were scheduled to pass through Maplewood on their way to a big city concert.

The news spread like wildfire. The Beatles, here, in Maplewood? It was almost too good to be true. The local radio station, usually reserved for farm reports and weather updates, played "I Want to Hold Your Hand" on repeat, while teenagers and even their parents were swept up in Beatlemania.

A makeshift stage was set up in the town park, and the whole community turned out, decked in their best 60s attire, holding handmade signs, and buzzing with excitement. Local bands played Beatles covers, the air was filled with the smell of barbecue and cotton candy, and the sense of anticipation was palpable.

As the Beatles' expected time of arrival drew near, a convoy of black cars appeared on the horizon. The crowd erupted in cheers, only to burst into laughter when out of the cars stepped not the Fab Four, but the Maplewood High School drama club, dressed as John, Paul, George, and Ringo. It turned out the real Beatles had taken a different route!

But the people of Maplewood weren't disappointed for long. The students took to the stage and performed with such enthusiasm and joy that it was as if the Beatles really had come to town. Couples danced, kids sang along, and for a few hours, Maplewood was the center of the rock 'n' roll universe.

That day became a cherished memory for the residents of Maplewood. It was a day filled with laughter, music, and community spirit, a reminder that sometimes, the best moments come from the unexpected and the joy of coming together, even if the Beatles never really came to town.

Did you know that before they became famous as The Beatles, the band experimented with various names including "The Quarrymen" and "Johnny and the Moondogs"? It wasn't until 1960 that they settled on the name "The Beatles," a play on words combining "beat" with "beetles" as a nod to Buddy Holly's band, The Crickets.

Did you know that later in life, John Lennon became an outspoken advocate for peace and social justice, using his fame to promote messages of love and unity? He and his wife Yoko Ono organized "Bed-Ins for Peace" in 1969 and 1970 as non-violent protests against war, and Lennon's song "Imagine" became an anthem for peace around the world.

Memory Lane

1960s Cultural Highlights

British Invasion in Music:

The 1960s marked a seismic shift in the music world with the British Invasion, led by The Beatles. Their arrival on American shores in 1964 changed everything, from fashion to music. The Beatles' catchy melodies, mop-top haircuts, and charismatic personalities captivated the hearts of millions. Remember when "I Want to Hold Your Hand" first played on the radio, and how it felt like the whole world suddenly started swaying to a new rhythm?

Cinema Revolution:

This decade witnessed a revolution in cinema, breaking traditional norms and exploring new thematic depths. Movies like "Psycho" challenged the conventional boundaries of filmmaking, while "2001: A Space Odyssey" took audiences on an unparalleled visual and cerebral journey. The rebellious spirit of the 60s was perfectly encapsulated in "Easy Rider," a film that became a symbol of freedom and counter-culture. These movies weren't just entertainment; they were mirrors reflecting a rapidly changing society.

Television's Golden Era:

The 1960s was a golden era for television, with groundbreaking shows that captured the essence of a changing world. "Star Trek" dared to imagine a future of diversity and exploration, "The Andy Griffith Show" offered a comforting glimpse of small-town life, and "Batman" brought comic book flamboyance to the small screen. These shows were more than just diversions; they were a part of everyday life, influencing and reflecting the moods of a vibrant decade.

Woodstock and the Hippie Movement:

In 1969, a music festival in upstate New York, known as Woodstock, became the epitome of the 60s hippie movement. It was more than a music festival; it was a symbol of peace, love, and communal living. Imagine the sight of hundreds of thousands gathered in harmony, swaying to the tunes of Jimi Hendrix, Janis Joplin, and The Who. Woodstock became a defining moment of the decade, a testament to the power of music and unity.

The Age of Space Exploration:

The 1960s was a decade that took humanity to new frontiers with the space race. The landmark moment came in 1969 when Apollo 11 landed on the moon, and Neil Armstrong took his "one small step for man, one giant leap for mankind." This

wasn't just a triumph for America; it was a monumental achievement for all humanity. The moon landing united people around the globe,

glued to their television sets, marveling at the boundless possibilities of human achievement. Do you remember where you were when mankind walked on the moon?

Did you know that Jimi Hendrix initially started his career as a backing guitarist before rising to fame as a solo artist?

Quiz Time

1960s Trivia Questions: The Swinging Sixties

Which music festival in 1969 became an emblem of the counterculture movement?

- Monterey Pop
- Festival Woodstock o
- Isle of Wight Festival

What was the popular fashion trend among women, characterized by very short skirts, in the 1960s?

- Maxi skirts
- Pencil skirts
- Mini skirts

Did you know that Bob Dylan originally gained fame as a folk musician before transitioning to rock music in the mid-1960s? His bold lyrics, distinctive voice, and poetic songwriting style have made him a cultural icon and earned him numerous accolades, including the Nobel Prize in Literature in 2016.

Which British band led the 'British Invasion' of the US music scene in the 1960s?

- The Beatles
- The Rolling Stones
- The Who

What was the name of the 1960s cultural movement that emphasized peace, love, and freedom?

- The Beat Generation
- The Hippie Movement
- The Punk Movement

In 1963, who delivered the famous "I Have a Dream" speech during the March on Washington?

- Malcolm X
- Martin Luther King Jr.
- Rosa Parks

Did you know that The Rolling Stones made their Super Bowl halftime show debut at Super Bowl XL in 2006?

Which 1960s television show is credited with breaking racial barriers by featuring the first interracial kiss on American TV?

- The Andy Griffith Show
- Star Trek
- I Spy

The Beatles' album 'Sgt. Pepper's Lonely Hearts Club Band' was released in what year?

- 1967
- 1962
- 1969

Which iconic event in 1969 marked the peak of the Civil Rights Movement?

- Martin Luther King Jr Assassination
- The Voting Rights Act
- The Stonewall Riots

Did you know that the iconic cover of "Sgt. Pepper's Lonely Hearts Club Band" by The Beatles features a collage of 57 famous people, including Marilyn Monroe, Albert Einstein, and Karl Marx

Who was the first man to walk on the moon in 1969?

- Neil Armstrong
- Buzz Aldrin
- Michael Collins

In which year did the first human spaceflight occur, conducted by the Soviet Union?

- A) 1961
- B) 1965
- C) 1969

Who was the first woman in space, achieving this feat in 1963?

- Sally Ride
- Valentina Tereshkova
- Mae Jemison

Did you know that in 2012, Buzz Aldrin became the oldest person to reach the South Pole at the age of 82? This remarkable expedition showcased Aldrin's adventurous spirit and determination to explore new frontiers even in his later years.

Which NASA program, starting in 1961, aimed to land humans on the Moon and bring them back safely to Earth?

- Apollo Program
- Gemini Program
- Mercury Program

In what year did the Apollo 11 mission successfully land on the Moon?

- 1969
- 1968
- 1967

Which spacecraft performed the first successful flyby of Mars in 1965?

- Mariner 4
- Viking 1
- Pioneer 10

Did you know that Mars, often called the "Red Planet" due to its reddish appearance, is named after the Roman god of war? This name was chosen because of the planet's reddish hue, which is caused by iron oxide, or rust, covering its surface.

What was the name of the first successful weather satellite launched in 1960?

- Nimbus-1
- TIROS-1
- GOES-1

Who shared the 1962 Nobel Prize in Physiology or Medicine for the discovery of the molecular structure of DNA?

- Linus Pauling Rosalind Franklin
- James Watson and Francis Crick

Which important environmental book, published in 1962, raised awareness about the effects of pesticides?

- Silent Spring
- The Population Bomb
- The Limits to Growth

Did you know that there are currently over 2,000 operational satellites orbiting the Earth, performing various functions such as communication, navigation, weather monitoring, and scientific research?

In 1967, the first human heart transplant was performed by which surgeon?

- Michael DeBakey
- Christiaan Barnard
- Denton Cooley

The first commercial communications satellite, Telstar, was launched in which year?

- 1960
- 1962
- 1965

Who was the famous leader of the Civil Rights Movement known for his philosophy of nonviolence and civil disobedience?

- Malcolm X
- Martin Luther King Jr.
- Thurgood Marshall

Did you know that Malcolm X changed his last name from Little to X to symbolize his lost African heritage, as X represents the unknown name given to his ancestors during slavery?

Which organization was founded by Martin Luther King Jr. in 1957 and became a leading force in the Civil Rights Movement?

- National Association for the Advancement of Colored People (NAACP)

- Southern Christian Leadership Conference (SCLC)

- Congress of Racial Equality (CORE)

The Historic Selma to Montgomery marches in 1965 were instrumental in leading to the passage of which Act?

- The Civil Rights Act of 1964

- The Voting Rights Act of 1965

- The Fair Housing Act

Who was the young African American boy whose brutal murder in Mississippi in 1955 became a catalyst for the Civil Rights Movement?

- Rodney King

- Emmett Till

- Medgar Evers

Which famous sit-in protest began at a Woolworth's lunch counter in Greensboro, North Carolina, in 1960?

- The Freedom Rides

- The Greensboro Sit-ins

- The Montgomery Bus Boycott

Who was the first African American student admitted to the University of Mississippi, a momentous event in 1962?

- Rosa Parks

- James Meredith

- Ruby Bridges

In 1967, Thurgood Marshall became the first African American to serve on what?

- The U.S. Senate

- The Supreme Court of the United States

- As a U.S. Presidential Advisor

Did you know that the U.S. Senate has a unique tradition called the "filibuster," which allows senators to speak for an extended period to delay or block legislation?

Did you know that the U.S. Senate, often referred to as the "upper chamber" of Congress, was originally designed to represent the interests of the individual states, with each state initially having two senators regardless of population size.

What was the name of the group founded by Bobby Seale and Huey Newton in 1966

- The Black Panther Party
- The African National Congress
- The Nation of Islam

Which band led the British Invasion into the American music scene in the early 1960s?

- The Beatles
- The Rolling Stones
- The Who

What was the name of the music festival in 1967, famously known as the 'Summer of Love'?

- Woodstock
- Monterey Pop Festival
- Isle of Wight Festival

Did you know that The Who's drummer, Keith Moon, once drove a car into a swimming pool as a prank? This incident, which occurred during a party at a Holiday Inn in Flint, Michigan, in the 1960s, became one of the legendary stories associated with Moon's wild antics.

Who performed the legendary rendition of "The Star-Spangled Banner" at Woodstock in 1969?

- Jimi Hendrix
- Janis Joplin
- Joe Cocker

Which song by The Rolling Stones, released in 1965, became one of their greatest hits?

- "Paint It Black"
- "Sympathy for the Devil"
- "Satisfaction"

Did you know that Mick Jagger, the lead singer of The Rolling Stones, was knighted by Queen Elizabeth II in 2003 for his services to music? Despite controversy surrounding his rebellious image, Jagger's knighthood recognized his significant contributions to the music industry and his enduring influence as a rock icon.

Bob Dylan famously transitioned from acoustic to electric guitar at which festival in 1965?

- Newport Folk
- Festival Woodstock
- Monterey Pop Festival

Which iconic album did The Beach Boys release in 1966?

- "Pet Sounds"
- "Surfin' USA"
- "California Girls"

What was the name of the first successful Motown group with hits like "My Girl"?

- The Supremes
- The Temptations
- The Four Tops

Did you know that Motown Records, founded by Berry Gordy Jr. in 1959, played a pivotal role in breaking racial barriers in the music industry by producing crossover hits that appealed to both black and white audiences

Who was the "Queen of Soul" in the 1960s, known for songs like "Respect"?

- Diana Ross

- Aretha Franklin

- Tina Turner

Did you know that Motown Records, founded by Berry Gordy Jr. in 1959, played a significant role in breaking down racial barriers in the music industry by producing crossover hits that appealed to both black and white audiences?

The song "Hotel California" was a hit for which band?

- The Eagles

- Fleetwood Mac

- Pink Floyd

Which crisis in 1962 marked the peak of tensions during the Cold War?

- Berlin Wall Collapse

- Cuban Missile Crisis

- Korean War

Who was the first U.S. President to resign from office, doing so in 1969 amid the Vietnam War controversy?

- John F. Kennedy

- Lyndon B. Johnson

- Richard Nixon

Did you know that Fidel Castro, the leader of the Cuban Revolution, held power in Cuba for nearly five decades, making him one of the longest-serving leaders in modern history?

The Vietnam War escalated significantly during the 1960s under which U.S. President?

- John F. Kennedy

- Lyndon B. Johnson

- Richard Nixon

In 1961, which country built a wall dividing its capital city, symbolizing the Cold War division between East and West?

- Germany

- Korea

- Vietnam

What significant event occurred in France in May 1968?

- The signing of the Treaty of Rome
- Student-led protests and general strikes
- The end of Charles de Gaulle's presidency

Did you know that Charles de Gaulle was wounded multiple times and captured by German forces during World War I? Despite enduring significant hardships as a prisoner of war, he managed to escape captivity multiple times.

In 1964, which African leader became the first Prime Minister of independent Tanzania?

- Jomo Kenyatta
- Kwame Nkrumah
- Julius Nyerere

Which pivotal civil rights legislation was signed into law by President Lyndon B. Johnson in 1965?

- Civil Rights Act
- Voting Rights
- Act Fair Housing Act

In 1967, which Middle Eastern conflict significantly altered the region's political landscape?

- Arab-Israeli War

- Six-Day War

- Yom Kippur War

Did you know that Tanzania is home to Mount Kilimanjaro, the highest peak in Africa? This majestic mountain attracts thousands of climbers and adventurers from around the world each year

Which treaty, signed in 1963, aimed to limit the testing of nuclear weapons?

- Treaty of Versailles

- Partial Nuclear Test Ban

- Treaty Non-Proliferation Treaty

The "Prague Spring," a period of political liberalization, occurred in 1968 in which country?

- Czechoslovakia

- Poland

- Hungary

Answers for Trivia 1960s

Question: Which music festival in 1969 became an emblem of the counterculture movement?

Answer: Woodstock ✓

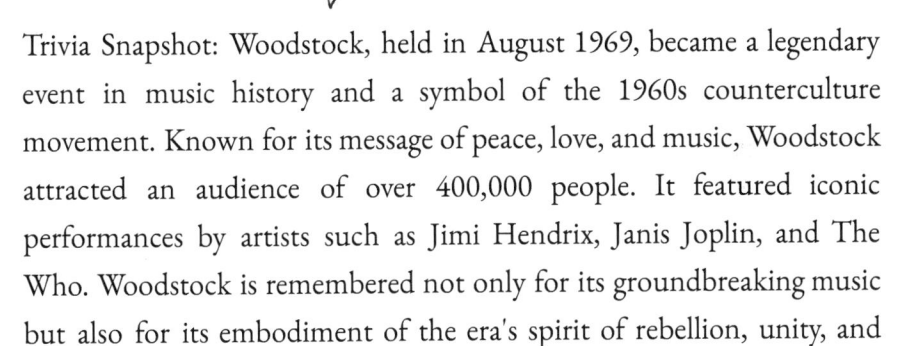

Trivia Snapshot: Woodstock, held in August 1969, became a legendary event in music history and a symbol of the 1960s counterculture movement. Known for its message of peace, love, and music, Woodstock attracted an audience of over 400,000 people. It featured iconic performances by artists such as Jimi Hendrix, Janis Joplin, and The Who. Woodstock is remembered not only for its groundbreaking music but also for its embodiment of the era's spirit of rebellion, unity, and social change.

Question: What was the popular fashion trend among women, characterized by very short skirts, in the 1960s?

Answer: Mini skirts ✓

Trivia Snapshot: The mini skirt, introduced in the early 1960s by designers like Mary Quant in London, quickly became a defining fashion trend of the decade. Characterized by its daringly short hemline, the mini skirt symbolized the youthful liberation and rebellious spirit of the time. It was seen as a form of self-expression and a break from traditional female fashion norms, aligning with the era's growing feminist movement.

Question: Which British band led the 'British Invasion' of the US music scene in the 1960s?

Answer: The Beatles

Trivia Snapshot: The Beatles, arguably the most influential band of the 20th century, spearheaded the British Invasion of the US music scene in the 1960s. Their appearance on "The Ed Sullivan Show" in 1964 marked a pivotal moment in American pop culture. The Beatles' innovative music, style, and charisma had a profound impact on the music industry and youth culture, setting new trends in music, fashion, and social attitudes.

Question: What was the name of the 1960s cultural movement that emphasized peace, love, and freedom?

Answer: The Hippie Movement

Trivia Snapshot: The Hippie Movement, which emerged in the mid-1960s, was a countercultural movement that rejected mainstream American life. The movement was characterized by its advocacy for peace, love, and personal freedom, often in opposition to the Vietnam War.

Hippies were known for their distinctive style, communal living, and alternative lifestyles. The movement reached its peak with events like the Summer of Love in 1967 and the Woodstock Festival in 1969, becoming a significant part of 1960s social history.

Question: In 1963, who delivered the famous "I Have a Dream" speech during the March on Washington?

Answer: Martin Luther King Jr.

Trivia Snapshot: Martin Luther King Jr.'s "I Have a Dream" speech, delivered during the March on Washington for Jobs and Freedom on August 28, 1963, is one of the most iconic speeches in American history. King's eloquent call for civil and economic rights and an end to racism in the United States became a defining moment of the Civil Rights Movement. The speech, delivered on the steps of the Lincoln Memorial, is celebrated for its powerful message of equality, freedom, and the pursuit of the American dream.

Question: Which 1960s television show is credited with breaking racial barriers by featuring the first interracial kiss on American TV?

Answer: Star Trek

Trivia Snapshot: "Star Trek," in its 1968 episode "Plato's Stepchildren," featured the first interracial kiss on American television between Captain Kirk, played by William Shatner, and Lieutenant Uhura, played by Nichelle Nichols. This groundbreaking moment was a significant step in challenging the racial norms of the time and reflected "Star Trek's" progressive approach to social issues. The show, created by Gene Roddenberry, is known for its portrayal of a diverse and inclusive future.

Question: The Beatles' album 'Sgt. Pepper's Lonely Hearts Club Band' was released in what year?

Answer: 1967

Trivia Snapshot: 'Sgt. Pepper's Lonely Hearts Club Band,' released by The Beatles in 1967, is often regarded as one of the most influential albums in the history of music. Known for its experimental sounds, innovative studio techniques, and elaborate cover art, the album marked a significant departure from traditional pop music. It won four Grammy

Awards and remains a landmark in the history of rock music, symbolizing the peak of the Beatles' creative collaboration.

Question: Which iconic event in 1969 marked the peak of the Civil Rights Movement?

Answer: The Stonewall Riots

Trivia Snapshot: The Stonewall Riots, which began in the early hours of June 28, 1969, at the Stonewall Inn in New York City, are widely considered a pivotal moment in the modern LGBTQ rights movement. The riots were a series of spontaneous demonstrations by members of the LGBTQ community in response to a police raid. These events marked a significant shift in the fight for LGBTQ rights in the United States, leading to the formation of various advocacy groups and the annual commemoration of Pride Month.

Question: Who was the first man to walk on the moon in 1969?

Answer: Neil Armstrong

Trivia Snapshot: Neil Armstrong became the first person to walk on the moon on July 20, 1969, during NASA's Apollo 11 mission. As he stepped onto the lunar surface, Armstrong famously aid, "That's one small step for man, one giant leap for mankind." This historic event was watched by millions of people around the world and represented a monumental achievement in human space exploration, fulfilling the United States' goal of landing a man on the moon and returning him safely to Earth.

Question: In which year did the first human spaceflight occur, conducted by the Soviet Union?

Answer: 1961

Trivia Snapshot: The first human spaceflight was achieved on April 12, 1961, by the Soviet Union with the Vostok 1 mission, carrying cosmonaut Yuri Gagarin. Gagarin became the first human to journey into outer space and orbit the Earth, marking a significant milestone in the Space Race and human space exploration. His famous words, "Poyekhali!" ("Let's go!"), and his orbit around the Earth made him an international hero and a symbol of Soviet space achievement.

Question: Who was the first woman in space, achieving this feat in 1963?

Answer: Valentina Tereshkova

Trivia Snapshot: Valentina Tereshkova, a Soviet cosmonaut, became the first woman to travel into space on June 16, 1963, aboard Vostok 6. Her mission made her an international icon and a symbol of women's contributions to space exploration. Tereshkova orbited the Earth 48 times, spent almost three days in space, and remains the only woman to have been on a solo space mission. Her journey was a major milestone in breaking gender barriers in the field of astronautics.

Question: Which NASA program, starting in 1961, aimed to land humans on the Moon and bring them back safely to Earth?

Answer: Apollo Program

Trivia Snapshot: The Apollo Program, initiated by NASA in 1961, was a series of space missions designed to land humans on the Moon and return them safely to Earth. This program was a response to President John F. Kennedy's 1961 challenge to land a man on the Moon before the decade's end. The Apollo missions not only achieved this goal but also advanced human space exploration, contributing significantly to our understanding of lunar geology and paving the way for future space exploration.

Question: In what year did the Apollo 11 mission successfully land on the Moon?

Answer: 1969

Trivia Snapshot: Apollo 11, the fifth manned mission of NASA's Apollo Program, made history on July 20, 1969, when astronauts Neil Armstrong and Buzz Aldrin became the first humans to land on the Moon. This mission fulfilled President Kennedy's goal and is remembered as one of humanity's greatest technological achievements. The iconic words of Neil Armstrong as he stepped onto the lunar surface, "That's one small step for [a] man, one giant leap for mankind," captured the monumental significance of the event.

Question: Which spacecraft performed the first successful flyby of Mars in 1965?

Answer: Mariner 4

Trivia Snapshot: Mariner 4, part of NASA's Mariner program, achieved the first successful flyby of Mars on July 14, 1965. This mission provided the first close-up images of the Martian surface, revealing a world of craters and unexpectedly barren landscapes. The success of Mariner 4 marked a significant milestone in interplanetary exploration and greatly expanded our knowledge of the Martian environment, laying the groundwork for future missions to explore the Red Planet.

Question: What was the name of the first successful weather satellite launched in 1960?

Answer: TIROS-1

Trivia Snapshot: TIROS-1 (Television Infrared Observation Satellite) was the world's first successful weather satellite, launched by NASA on April 1, 1960. This satellite revolutionized meteorology by providing the first accurate weather forecasts based on data gathered from space. TIROS-1 transmitted thousands of images back to Earth, offering unprecedented views of cloud cover and weather patterns, and laid the foundation for the development of modern meteorological satellite systems.

Question: Who shared the 1962 Nobel Prize in Physiology or Medicine for the discovery of the molecular structure of DNA?

Answer: James Watson and Francis Crick

Trivia Snapshot: James Watson and Francis Crick were awarded the Nobel Prize in Physiology or Medicine in 1962, along with Maurice Wilkins, for their discovery of the molecular structure of DNA. Their work on the double helix model of DNA was a monumental breakthrough in biology and genetics. This discovery not only deepened the understanding of genetic inheritance but also paved the way for modern biotechnology and genetic engineering.

Question: Which important environmental book, published in 1962, raised awareness about the effects of pesticides? Answer: A) Silent Spring

Trivia Snapshot: "Silent Spring," written by Rachel Carson and published in 1962, is considered one of the most influential environmental books ever written. The book exposed the dangers of indiscriminate pesticide use, particularly DDT, on wildlife and human health. Its publication led to a significant shift in public awareness about environmental issues and played a key role in the environmental movement, eventually leading to policy changes and the banning of DDT in the United States.

Question: In 1967, the first human heart transplant was performed by which surgeon?

Answer: Christiaan Barnard

Trivia Snapshot: Dr. Christiaan Barnard, a South African surgeon, performed the world's first successful human heart transplant on December 3, 1967. The groundbreaking operation took place at Groote Schuur Hospital in Cape Town, South Africa. This medical milestone opened the door to the field of organ transplantation, revolutionizing the treatment of severe heart disease and inspiring advancements in transplant medicine. Dr. Barnard's achievement was a testament to the possibilities of modern surgery and medical innovation.

Question: The first commercial communications satellite, Telstar, was launched in which year?

Answer: 1962

Trivia Snapshot: Telstar, the first commercial communications satellite, was launched on July 10, 1962. Developed by Bell Telephone Laboratories and launched by NASA, Telstar facilitated the first live transatlantic television broadcasts. This groundbreaking satellite revolutionized global communications, enabling not only television transmissions but also telephone and high-speed data services. Telstar's success marked the beginning of a new era in telecommunications, significantly impacting media, business, and personal communications.

Question: Who was the famous leader of the Civil Rights Movement known for his philosophy of nonviolence and civil disobedience?

Answer: Martin Luther King Jr.

Trivia Snapshot: Martin Luther King Jr. was a pivotal figure in the American Civil Rights Movement, renowned for his advocacy of nonviolence and civil disobedience. Inspired by Mahatma Gandhi's principles, King's leadership in the Montgomery Bus Boycott, the

Birmingham Campaign, and the March on Washington, where he delivered his iconic "I Have a Dream" speech, played a vital role in the movement's success. King's efforts led to significant legal and social changes in the United States, and his legacy continues to inspire movements for social justice and equality worldwide.

Question: In which city did the pivotal Civil Rights event known as the 'March on Washington for Jobs and Freedom' take place in 1963?

Answer: Washington, D.C.

Trivia Snapshot: The March on Washington for Jobs and Freedom, one of the largest political rallies for human rights in United States history, took place on August 28, 1963, in Washington,

C. Attended by approximately 250,000 people, the march aimed to advocate for civil and economic rights for African Americans. It was at this event that Martin Luther King Jr. delivered his historic "I Have a Dream" speech at the Lincoln Memorial. The march was a pivotal moment in the Civil Rights Movement and helped to galvanize efforts that led to the passage of the Civil Rights Act of 1964 and the Voting Rights Act of 1965.

Question: Which Act, passed in 1964, outlawed discrimination based on race, color, religion, sex, or national origin?

Answer: The Civil Rights Act of 1964

Trivia Snapshot: The Civil Rights Act of 1964, one of the most significant pieces of civil rights legislation in American history, was enacted on July 2, 1964. This landmark law prohibited discrimination on the basis of race, color, religion, sex, or national origin in employment practices and public accommodations. The Act also ended unequal application of voter registration requirements and racial segregation in schools, workplaces, and facilities that served the general public. The Civil Rights Act was a major victory for the Civil Rights Movement and a crucial step in the fight for equal rights in the United States.

Question: Which organization was founded by Martin Luther King Jr. in 1957 and became a leading force in the Civil Rights Movement?

Answer: Southern Christian Leadership Conference (SCLC)

Trivia Snapshot: The Southern Christian Leadership Conference (SCLC) was founded in 1957 by Martin Luther King Jr. and other civil rights leaders. The SCLC played a crucial role in the American Civil Rights Movement, with a focus on nonviolent protest and civil disobedience.

Under King's leadership, the SCLC organized some of the most significant campaigns of the Civil Rights Movement, including the Birmingham Campaign and the Selma to Montgomery marches. The organization aimed to harness the moral authority and organizing power of black churches to conduct nonviolent protests against the injustices of segregation.

Question: The historic Selma to Montgomery marches in 1965 were instrumental in leading to the passage of which Act?

Answer: The Voting Rights Act of 1965

Trivia Snapshot: The Selma to Montgomery marches, a series of three protest marches held in 1965, were pivotal in the struggle for voting rights for African Americans. These marches were a response to the barriers preventing black citizens from exercising their right to vote, especially in the South. The violence inflicted on marchers during the first march, known as "Bloody Sunday," drew national attention to the civil rights movement. The marches significantly influenced public opinion and led to the passage of the Voting Rights Act of 1965, landmark legislation that prohibited racial discrimination in voting. This Act is considered one of the most far-reaching pieces of civil rights legislation in U.S. history.

Question: Who was the young African American boy whose brutal murder in Mississippi in 1955 became a catalyst for the Civil Rights Movement?

Answer: Emmett Till

Trivia Snapshot: Emmett Till was a 14-year-old African American boy from Chicago who was brutally murdered while visiting relatives in Mississippi in 1955. His death became a galvanizing moment in the Civil Rights Movement after his mother, Mamie Till-Mobley, insisted on a public, open-casket funeral to show the world the horrors of racial violence. The images of his mutilated body published in the press and the subsequent acquittal of his killers ignited widespread outrage and activism, marking a significant turning point in the struggle for civil rights in

America.

Question: Which famous sit-in protest began at a Woolworth's lunch counter in Greensboro, North Carolina, in 1960?

Answer: The Greensboro Sit-ins

Trivia Snapshot: The Greensboro Sit-ins were a series of nonviolent protests that started on February 1, 1960, when four African American college students sat down at a segregated lunch counter at a Woolworth's store in Greensboro, North

Carolina, and politely asked for service. Their refusal to leave when denied service sparked a youth-led movement that spread to other southern states, challenging racial segregation in public facilities. The sit-ins played a crucial

role in the Civil Rights Movement and led to the formation of the Student Nonviolent Coordinating Committee (SNCC), one of the movement's most important organizations.

Question: Who was the first African American student admitted to the University of Mississippi, a momentous event in 1962?

Answer: James Meredith

Trivia Snapshot: James Meredith was the first African American student to enroll at the

University of Mississippi, a historic moment in the American Civil Rights Movement. His admission in 1962 was met with violent riots, requiring federal intervention to uphold his rights.

President John F. Kennedy sent federal troops to quell the riots and ensure Meredith's safety. Meredith's enrollment at the university was a significant challenge to racial segregation and a pivotal moment in the struggle for civil rights, symbolizing the federal government's commitment to enforcing court-ordered desegregation.

Question: Which band led the British Invasion into the American music scene in the early 1960s?

Answer: The Beatles

Trivia Snapshot: The Beatles were at the forefront of the British Invasion, a phenomenon in the early 1960s where British rock and pop music bands became immensely popular in the United States. The Beatles' appearance on "The Ed Sullivan Show" in February 1964 marked the beginning of this cultural phenomenon. Their unique sound, style, and charisma captivated American audiences and influenced countless artists. The Beatles' success in the U.S. opened the door for other British bands, transforming the global music scene.

Question: What was the name of the music festival in 1967, famously known as the 'Summer of Love'?

Answer: Monterey Pop Festival

Trivia Snapshot: The Monterey Pop Festival, held in June 1967 in Monterey, California, was a landmark event in the 1960s counterculture movement and is often associated with the 'Summer of Love.' This festival is notable for being one of the first major gatherings of the counterculture era and for featuring performances by some of the era's most influential musicians, including Janis Joplin, The Who, and Jimi

Hendrix. It set the stage for future music festivals, including Woodstock, and highlighted the rising influence of the youth culture.

Question: Who performed the legendary rendition of "The Star-Spangled Banner" at Woodstock in 1969?

Answer: Jimi Hendrix

Trivia Snapshot: Jimi Hendrix's performance of "The Star-Spangled Banner" at the Woodstock Music Festival in August 1969 is one of the most iconic moments in music history. His electrifying guitar rendition of the U.S. national anthem was a powerful and transformative interpretation that reflected the turbulent social and political atmosphere of the time.

Hendrix's performance at Woodstock, particularly this rendition, solidified his status as one of the greatest guitarists of all time.

Question: Which song by The Rolling Stones, released in 1965, became one of their greatest hits?

Answer: "Satisfaction"

Trivia Snapshot: "Satisfaction," released by The Rolling Stones in 1965, quickly became one of the band's most famous songs and a defining track of the rock genre. Known officially as "(I Can't Get No) Satisfaction," the song's distinctive guitar riff, rebellious spirit, and Mick Jagger's expressive vocals captured the mood of a generation. The song's success cemented The Rolling Stones' status as one of the leading bands of the rock era and remains a staple of their live performances.

Question: Bob Dylan famously transitioned from acoustic to electric guitar at which festival in 1965?

Answer: Newport Folk Festival

Trivia Snapshot: Bob Dylan's performance at the Newport Folk Festival in 1965 was a pivotal moment in music history. Known for his acoustic folk music, Dylan surprised and divided the audience by playing with an electric guitar and backed by a full band. This bold move marked a significant transition in his musical style and influenced the direction of folk and rock music.

Dylan's performance at Newport is often seen as symbolic of the changing times and the evolving nature of the music scene in the 1960s.

Question: Which iconic album did The Beach Boys release in 1966?

Answer: "Pet Sounds"

Trivia Snapshot: "Pet Sounds," released by The Beach Boys in 1966, is widely considered one of the most influential albums in the history of music. With its innovative production techniques, complex harmonies, and introspective lyrics, the album marked a significant departure from the band's earlier surf rock style. Produced by Brian Wilson, "Pet Sounds" was critically acclaimed for its artistic achievement and was instrumental in the evolution of pop music as an art form.

Question: What was the name of the first successful Motown group with hits like "My Girl"?

Answer: The Temptations

Trivia Snapshot: The Temptations, one of the most successful groups to come out of the Motown movement, are famous for hits like "My Girl," released in 1964. Known for their smooth harmonies, choreographed dance moves, and dapper suits, The Temptations played a significant role in defining the Motown sound. Their music, characterized by a blend of R&B, soul, and pop, left a lasting impact on the music industry and popular culture.

Question: Who was the "Queen of Soul" in the 1960s, known for songs like "Respect"?

Answer: Aretha Franklin

Trivia Snapshot: Aretha Franklin, often referred to as the "Queen of Soul," was one of the most influential and revered singers of the 20th century. Known for her powerful voice and emotive delivery, Franklin's music spanned a variety of genres, including soul, R&B, gospel, and pop.

Her 1967 hit "Respect," originally written and performed by Otis Redding, became an anthem for civil rights and feminist empowerment. Franklin's remarkable talent and her contributions to music and culture have made her an enduring icon.

Question: The song "Hotel California" was a hit for which band?

Answer: The Eagles

Trivia Snapshot: "Hotel California," released by The Eagles in 1976, is one of the band's most famous and enduring songs. Featured on the album of the same name, "Hotel California" is known for its distinctive guitar riff and enigmatic lyrics, which have been subject to various interpretations. The song won the 1977 Grammy Award for Record of the Year and remains a classic of the rock genre, showcasing The Eagles' signature blend of rock, country, and folk influences.

Question: Which crisis in 1962 marked the peak of tensions during the Cold War?

Answer: Cuban Missile Crisis

Trivia Snapshot: The Cuban Missile Crisis, a 13-day confrontation in October 1962 between the United States and the Soviet Union, is considered the closest the Cold War came to escalating into a full-scale nuclear war. Triggered by the Soviet installation of nuclear missiles in Cuba, just 90 miles from U.S. shores, the crisis was a critical moment of tension and brinkmanship. The resolution of the crisis, involving a secret agreement between U.S. President John F. Kennedy and Soviet Premier Nikita Khrushchev, led to the removal of the missiles and is often cited as an example of successful crisis management and diplomacy.

Question: Who was the first U.S. President to resign from office, doing so in 1969 amid the Vietnam War controversy?

Answer: Richard Nixon

Trivia Snapshot: Richard Nixon, the 37th President of the United States, became the first and only

U.S. President to resign from office, but his resignation occurred in 1974, not 1969. Nixon's resignation came amid the Watergate scandal, where he faced almost certain impeachment due to his involvement in the Watergate break-in and subsequent cover-up. While Nixon did escalate the Vietnam War early in his presidency, his resignation was primarily due to the domestic political crisis stemming from Watergate.

Question: The Vietnam War escalated significantly during the 1960s under which U.S. President?

Answer: Lyndon B. Johnson

Trivia Snapshot: The Vietnam War escalated significantly under U.S. President Lyndon B. Johnson, who took office following the assassination of John F. Kennedy in 1963. Johnson's administration saw a substantial increase in U.S. military involvement in Vietnam, following the Gulf of Tonkin Resolution in 1964. His decision to deploy more troops and resources to the conflict was a key factor in the war's intensification, leading to increased American casualties and growing anti-war sentiment both in the United States and around the world.

Question: In 1961, which country built a wall dividing its capital city, symbolizing the Cold War division between East and West?

Answer: Germany

Trivia Snapshot: The Berlin Wall, constructed in 1961 by East Germany (GDR), divided the city of Berlin into East and West sections. It became a stark symbol of the Cold War, representing the ideological divide between the communist East and the democratic West. The Wall was built to prevent East Germans from fleeing to the West and stood for nearly three decades. Its fall in 1989 signaled the end of the Cold War and the beginning of German reunification.

Question: What significant event occurred in France in May 1968?

Answer: Student-led protests and general strikes

Trivia Snapshot: May 1968 in France was marked by a series of student-led protests, general strikes, and civil unrest. What started as a movement for educational reform quickly escalated

Trivia Snapshot: The Partial Nuclear Test Ban Treaty, signed in 1963, was an agreement between the United States, the Soviet Union, and the

United Kingdom to prohibit nuclear weapons tests in the atmosphere, in outer space, and under water. The treaty was a response

to growing concerns about radioactive fallout from atmospheric nuclear tests and represented a significant step towards nuclear disarmament and the prevention of nuclear proliferation. It paved the way for future arms control agreements.

Question: The "Prague Spring," a period of political liberalization, occurred in 1968 in which country?

Answer: Czechoslovakia

Trivia Snapshot: The "Prague Spring" was a period of political liberalization and reform in Czechoslovakia during 1968 under the leadership of Alexander Dubček. This movement sought to create "socialism with a human face" through reforms that included loosening restrictions on the media, speech, and travel. However, the Prague Spring was abruptly ended when the Soviet Union and other members of the Warsaw Pact invaded Czechoslovakia in August 1968, enforcing a return to orthodox socialist rule. The event had significant implications for the Cold War and the policy of détente between the East and the West.

1970s

The Disco Decade

Story TIme

Title: Disco Fever at the Senior Center

In the heart of 1978, in the bustling town of Springfield, the local senior center decided to shake things up. With disco at its peak, Mrs. Gladys, the spirited activities director, thought it was high time the seniors got a taste of the disco mania that had taken over the country. She announced a 'Disco Night' much to the bemusement and curiosity of the center's regulars.

As the big night approached, the center transformed. A glittering disco ball was hung, and colorful lights were strung up. The seniors, initially skeptical, began to warm up to the idea, digging out wide- collar shirts and polyester dresses from the backs of their closets.

The evening kicked off with some hesitation – feet shuffled, hands clapped off-beat, and there were more than a few raised eyebrows. But then, something magical happened. When the DJ played "Stayin' Alive" by the Bee Gees, Mr. Jenkins, a quiet widower known for his cardigan sweaters, suddenly burst into a surprisingly nimble rendition of the hustle.

Laughter and cheers erupted. Soon, everyone was on the dance floor, from Mrs. Robinson, who hadn't danced since her high school prom, to

Bob and Linda, who discovered they could still boogie like it was 1959. The room was alive with energy, swaying hips, and beaming smiles.

As the night drew to a close with Donna Summer's "Last Dance," the seniors were reluctant to leave the floor. It was an evening where they forgot their ages, relived their youth, and discovered that disco wasn't just for the young. The Disco Fever Night became a legend at the center, a night of unexpected joy and revival, proving that age is just a number and rhythm lives in everyone's heart.

Did you know that in 1979, the Sony Walkman portable cassette player was introduced, allowing people to listen to music on the go for the first time? This innovative device transformed the way people experienced music and became an iconic symbol of 1970s pop culture.

Did you know that in 1973, the film "Enter the Dragon" was released, starring Bruce Lee in his final role before his untimely death? This martial arts masterpiece helped popularize kung fu cinema around the world and solidified Lee's status as a cultural icon.

Did you know that in 1978, the first test-tube baby, Louise Brown, was born, marking a major breakthrough in reproductive science and paving the way for advancements in fertility treatments?

Memory Lane
1970s Cultural Highlights Disco Craze:

The 1970s will forever be remembered as the era of disco. The pulsating beats of disco music filled dance floors across the world. From the iconic "Saturday Night Fever" soundtrack to

Donna Summer's electric performances, disco was more than a music genre; it was a cultural phenomenon. Remember the glitter balls, the flamboyant outfits, and the joy of dancing the night away under neon lights? Disco was an escape, a celebration of life and freedom expressed through dance.

Blockbuster Movies:

This decade saw the rise of blockbuster movies, changing the face of cinema. "Jaws" terrified and thrilled audiences in equal measure, "Star Wars" launched a saga that captured the imaginations of millions, and "Rocky" told a story of perseverance that resonated with many. These films were more than mere entertainment; they were shared experiences that brought people together, often in long lines outside cinemas, eagerly awaiting the next cinematic adventure.

Television's Evolving Landscape:

Television in the 1970s evolved to reflect the changing social landscape. "All in the Family" tackled previously taboo subjects, "MAS*H" mixed comedy with poignant social commentary, and "Happy Days" brought nostalgia for simpler times. These shows were more than just popular entertainment; they were windows into society, offering both escapism and a mirror to the world outside.

Environmental Awakening:

The 1970s marked a critical turning point in environmental awareness. The first Earth Day in 1970 awakened a global consciousness about the planet. This decade also saw the passage of significant environmental legislation and the formation of influential environmental groups.

Remember how the conversation shifted, from treating the planet as an inexhaustible resource to a precious home that needed care and protection?

The Glam Rock Movement:

Music in the 70s also saw the emergence of Glam Rock. Artists like David Bowie, with his alter ego Ziggy Stardust, and bands like Queen broke the mold with their theatrical performances and androgynous fashion. This wasn't just a musical trend; it was an artistic expression that challenged traditional norms and inspired a generation to embrace individuality and flamboyance.

1970s Trivia Questions: Disco and Fashion

Which movie, starring John Travolta, epitomized the disco culture and fashion of the 1970s?

- Saturday Night

- Fever Grease

- Staying Alive

What iconic fashion item, characterized by a flared bottom and often worn at disco clubs, was popular in the 1970s?

- Bell-bottom pants
- Mini skirts
- Poodle skirts

Which dance move, involving pointing a finger in the air and then towards the floor, became synonymous with the disco era?

- The Hustle
- The Bump
- The Funky Chicken

Who was known as the 'Queen of Disco' in the 1970s for hits like 'I Feel Love'?

- Diana Ross
- Donna Summer
- Gloria Gaynor

Did you know that John Travolta is a prominent member of the Church of Scientology? Travolta has been associated with the controversial religious movement since the 1970s.

Which footwear, characterized by thick soles, became a fashion staple during the disco era?

- Platform shoes

- Go-go boots

- Ballet flats

Which fashion designer is credited with popularizing the wrap dress in the 1970s?

- Vivienne Westwood

- Diane von Fürstenberg

- Coco Chanel

What was the name of the famous New York City nightclub that became a cultural icon of the disco era?

- The Cotton Club

- Studio 54

- CBGB

Did you know that in the 1970s, New York City became the birthplace of modern graffiti and street art movements, with artists like Keith Haring and Jean-Michel Basquiat gaining prominence for their innovative and expressive works in public spaces?

Which 1970s TV show is credited with bringing disco music and dance to mainstream America?

- Soul Train

- Bandstand

What was the primary goal of the Clean Air Act, significantly amended in 1970?

- To reduce greenhouse gas emissions

- To control air pollution on a national level

- To promote renewable energy

What environmental disaster occurred in 1979, leading to a significant nuclear accident?

- Chernobyl disaster

- Three Mile Island accident

- Fukushima Daiichi nuclear disaster

Did you know that today, the Chernobyl Exclusion Zone has become an unexpected haven for wildlife, with thriving populations of animals such as wolves, deer, and even endangered species like the Eurasian lynx?

Which term, coined in the 1970s, refers to a proposed geological epoch recognizing human impact on Earth's ecosystems?

- Anthropocene

- Holocene Eocene

In 1979, which international treaty was signed to protect the ozone layer?

- Montreal Protocol

- Vienna Convention for the Protection of the Ozone Layer

- The Rio Earth Summit

Key Historical Events Which U.S. President resigned in 1974 due to the Watergate scandal?

- Richard Nixon

- Gerald Ford

The Vietnam War ended in 1975 with the fall of which city?

- Hanoi

- Ho Chi Minh City (Saigon)

- Hue

Which country's revolution in 1979 led to the establishment of an Islamic Republic?

- Afghanistan

- Iran

- Iraq

What was the main purpose of the Camp David Accords signed in 1978?

- To end the Vietnam War

- To establish peace between Israel and Egypt

- To start the European Union

In 1971, which country was divided into two, leading to the creation of Bangladesh?

- India

- Pakistan

- Sri Lanka

Did you know that Mahatma Gandhi practiced nonviolent resistance as a means of achieving social and political change? His philosophy of "Satyagraha" (truth-force) inspired civil rights movements around the world and earned him the title of "Father of the Nation" in India.

Who became the first female Prime Minister of a major Western power in 1979?

- Indira Gandhi

- Golda Meir

- Margaret Thatcher

Which landmark U.S. Supreme Court decision in 1973 ruled that abortion rights fall within the privacy guaranteed by the 14th Amendment?

- Brown v. Board of Education

- Roe v. Wade

The Munich massacre, involving the hostage-taking of Israeli Olympic team members, occurred during which Olympic Games?

- 1972 Munich

- 1976 Montreal

- 1980 Moscow

Did you know that Margaret Thatcher grew up in a modest household in Grantham, Lincolnshire? Despite her humble beginnings, Thatcher's parents instilled in her a strong work ethic and a belief in self-reliance, values that would shape her political career and influence her conservative ideology.

In 1972, President Richard Nixon made a historic visit to which country, significantly altering Cold War dynamics?

- Soviet Union
- China
- Vietnam

The first test-tube baby was born in 1978 in which country?

- United States
- United Kingdom
- Sweden

Which 1975 movie, directed by Steven Spielberg, is often credited as the first major summer blockbuster?

- Jaws
- Star Wars
- Rocky

Did you know that Vietnam is home to one of the world's largest cave systems, including the breathtaking Son Doong Cave? Discovered in 1991 and officially explored in 2009, Son Doong is considered the largest cave in the world by volume and features stunning limestone formations, underground rivers, and unique ecosystems.

Who directed the 1972 crime film 'The Godfather'?

- Francis Ford Coppola
- Martin Scorsese
- Alfred Hitchcock

Which science fiction film released in 1977 became a cultural phenomenon and spawned a major franchise?

- Close Encounters of the
- Third Kind Alien
- Star Wars

What was the name of the first African American to win an Academy Award for Best Actor, which he received in 1964 for 'Lilies of the Field'?

- Sidney Poitier
- Morgan Freeman
- Denzel Washington

Did you know that Alfred Hitchcock made cameo appearances in almost all of his films? These brief appearances became a trademark of Hitchcock's work, with audiences eagerly anticipating his subtle cameos as they watched his thrilling movies.

Which 1976 movie featured Robert De Niro's famous line, "You talkin' to me?"

- Taxi Driver

- Raging Bull

The 1970s saw the rise of martial arts films. Which actor became synonymous with this genre?

- huck Norris

- Bruce Lee

- Jackie Chan

What film won the Academy Award for Best Picture in 1979?

- Apocalypse Now

- Kramer vs. Kramer

- The Deer Hunter

Did you know that in "Taxi Driver," Martin Scorsese employed a unique filmmaking technique called "guerrilla-style" shooting, capturing authentic footage of New York City streets without permits or permissions? This approach allowed Scorsese to create a gritty, realistic portrayal of urban life, immersing audiences in the seedy underbelly of 1970s Manhattan.

Which movie musical set in the 1950s and starring John Travolta and Olivia Newton-John became a huge hit in 1978?

- Grease
- Hair Spray
- Tick Tick Boom

Which horror film, directed by William Friedkin in 1973, became one of the most profitable horror movies ever made?

- The Exorcist
- The Texas Chain Saw Massacre
- Halloween

In the 1979 film 'Alien,' who played the character of Ellen Ripley?

- Sigourney Weaver
- Meryl Streep
- Jodie Foster

Did you know that Olivia Newton-John, in addition to her successful music career, is also an avid environmental activist and entrepreneur? She co-owns a wellness retreat center in Australia and has released multiple albums focused on healing and mindfulness.

Answers for Trivia 1970s

Question: Which movie, starring John Travolta, epitomized the disco culture and fashion of the 1970s?

Answer: Saturday Night Fever

Trivia Snapshot: "Saturday Night Fever," released in 1977 and starring John Travolta, became a cultural phenomenon and a defining film of the 1970s disco era. The movie showcased the vibrant disco scene and its influence on fashion, music, and dance. Travolta's character, Tony Manero, with his slick dance moves and iconic white suit, became a symbol of the disco culture. The film's soundtrack, featuring hits by the Bee Gees, played a significant role in popularizing disco music worldwide.

Question: What iconic fashion item, characterized by a flared bottom and often worn at disco clubs, was popular in the 1970s?

Answer: Bell-bottom pants

Trivia Snapshot: Bell-bottom pants, characterized by their flared bottoms, were a quintessential fashion item of the 1970s. Originally derived from naval uniforms, they became popular in mainstream fashion and were a staple at disco clubs. Paired with platform shoes and vibrant patterns, bell-bottoms embodied the flamboyant and expressive style of the disco era. Their popularity marked a shift in fashion towards more individualistic and unconventional styles.

Question: Which dance move, involving pointing a finger in the air and then towards the floor, became synonymous with the disco era?

Answer: The Hustle

Trivia Snapshot: The Hustle became one of the most popular dance moves of the 1970s disco era. This dance, often associated with Van McCoy's 1975 hit "The Hustle," involved a series of steps and turns, including the distinctive move of pointing a finger in the air and then towards the floor. The Hustle captured the essence of disco dancing with its upbeat, syncopated rhythms and became a staple in discotheques across the world.

Question: Who was known as the 'Queen of Disco' in the 1970s for hits like 'I Feel Love'?

Answer: Donna Summer

Trivia Snapshot: Donna Summer, often referred to as the "Queen of Disco," was one of the most influential and successful artists of the disco era. Her innovative music, which blended electronic sounds with soulful vocals, defined the sound of the 1970s disco movement. Hits like "I Feel Love," "Love to Love You Baby," and "Last Dance" showcased her powerful voice and the evolving electronic production techniques of the time. Summer's impact on disco music and her role in shaping the genre earned her widespread acclaim and a lasting legacy in the music industry.

Question: Which footwear, characterized by thick soles, became a fashion staple during the disco era?

Answer: Platform shoes

Trivia Snapshot: Platform shoes, known for their thick soles and high heels, became a defining fashion item of the 1970s, particularly during the disco era. These shoes were popular among both men and women and complemented the flamboyant and expressive style of the time. Worn on dance floors and in everyday life, platform shoes not only added height but also an element of drama and glamour to the wearer's outfit, embodying the bold and extravagant fashion trends of the decade.

Question: Which fashion designer is credited with popularizing the wrap dress in the 1970s?

Answer: Diane von Fürstenberg

Trivia Snapshot: Diane von Fürstenberg is credited with popularizing the wrap dress in the 1970s. This versatile and elegant garment, known for its simplicity, comfort, and flattering fit, became a symbol of women's liberation and empowerment. The wrap dress's easy-to-wear style, with a front closure formed by wrapping one side across the other, made it a staple in women's wardrobes. Its popularity endures today, showcasing von Fürstenberg's lasting impact on women's fashion.

Question: What was the name of the famous New York City nightclub that became a cultural icon of the disco era?

Answer: Studio 54

Trivia Snapshot: Studio 54, located in New York City, was the epitome of the disco era's extravagant nightlife. Opening in 1977, it quickly became known for its celebrity clientele, extravagant parties, and wild atmosphere. Studio 54 was more than just a nightclub; it was a symbol of the era's glamorous and hedonistic lifestyle. The club's mix of music, fashion, and celebrity culture made it a legendary spot in the history of nightlife and disco.

Question: Which 1970s TV show is credited with bringing disco music and dance to mainstream America?

Answer: B) Soul Train

Trivia Snapshot: "Soul Train," which first aired in 1971, played a significant role in bringing disco music and dance to mainstream America. Created by Don Cornelius, the show was a showcase for R&B, soul, and later disco music, featuring performances by major artists and dance segments by the show's audience. "Soul Train" was not only influential in popularizing disco music but also in celebrating African American culture and style, becoming an iconic platform for new music and dance trends.

Question: Which group's 1977 album 'Saturday Night Fever' became one of the best-selling albums of all time?

Answer: The Bee Gees

Trivia Snapshot: The Bee Gees' soundtrack album for the 1977 film "Saturday Night Fever" played a crucial role in popularizing disco music across the globe. Featuring hits like "Stayin' Alive," "How Deep Is Your Love," and "Night Fever," the album became one of the best-selling albums of all time. Its impact on the music industry was immense, defining the disco era and influencing the development of dance music in the subsequent decades. The album's success also cemented the Bee Gees' status as icons of the disco genre.

Question: What hairstyle, characterized by feathered layers, became popular among both men and women in the disco era?

Answer: The Shag

Trivia Snapshot: The shag haircut, characterized by its feathered layers and often a tousled look, became a popular hairstyle among both men and women in the 1970s. This asy-to-maintain and versatile hairstyle reflected the era's laid-back yet stylish aesthetic. Celebrities like Farrah Fawcett and David Bowie popularized the shag, making it one of the signature looks of the disco era and a trend that has seen various revivals in the fashion world.

Question: In what year was the first personal computer, the Altair 8800, introduced?

Answer: 1975

Trivia Snapshot: The Altair 8800, introduced in 1975, is widely recognized as the first commercially successful personal computer. Created by Micro Instrumentation and Telemetry Systems (MITS), the Altair 8800 appealed to computer hobbyists and helped spark the personal computing revolution. The Altair's release was a significant milestone in computing history, paving the way for the development of more user-friendly personal computers and the growth of companies like Microsoft and Apple.

Question: Which company released the popular video game 'Pong' in 1972?

Answer: Atari

Trivia Snapshot: "Pong," released by Atari in 1972, was one of the first video games to gain widespread popularity, both in arcades and later as a home console game. This simple table tennis simulation game was a pioneer in the video gaming industry and played a significant role in establishing video games as a mainstream form of entertainment. The success of "Pong" marked the beginning of the commercial video game industry and Atari's rise as a key player in the field.

Question: Who is credited with inventing the first microprocessor in 1971?

Answer: Intel

Trivia Snapshot: Intel is credited with inventing the first commercially available microprocessor, the Intel 4004, in 1971. This groundbreaking invention, a complete central processing unit on a single chip, revolutionized the electronics industry. The microprocessor's development marked the beginning of the digital age, enabling the creation of smaller, more powerful, and more affordable computers and a wide array of electronic devices. The Intel 4004 laid the foundation for the modern computing and electronics industry.

Question: The Sony Walkman, a revolutionary portable music player, was released in which year? Answer: C) 1979

Trivia Snapshot: The Sony Walkman, introduced in 1979, revolutionized the way people listened to music on the go. This portable cassette player allowed users to listen to music through headphones while walking, commuting, or engaging in outdoor activities, making personal, portable music a reality for the first time. The Walkman's compact design and functionality marked a significant shift in music consumption habits and influenced the development of portable media and listening devices in the years to come.

Question: Which technological innovation, first introduced in the 1970s, revolutionized the way people listened to music at home?

Answer: The Cassette Tape

Trivia Snapshot: The cassette tape, introduced in the 1970s, became a popular medium for recording and listening to music. Its compact size and the ability to record and playback easily made it a preferable alternative to vinyl records and 8- track tapes. The cassette tape's portability and the advent of portable cassette players like the Sony Walkman further enhanced its popularity. This innovation played a key role in the democratization of music listening and recording, influencing music culture and consumption.

Question: What was the name of the first commercially successful home video game console released in 1972?

Answer: Magnavox Odyssey

Trivia Snapshot: The Magnavox Odyssey, released in 1972, was the first commercially successful home video game console. Designed by Ralph Baer, known as the "Father of Video Games," the Odyssey was a pioneering device that played a variety of simple games on a television screen, including a primitive form of table tennis that predated Atari's "Pong." Although rudimentary by today's standards, the Magnavox Odyssey represented the birth of the home video game industry and laid the groundwork for future advancements in gaming technology.

Question: The first mobile phone call was made in 1973 by an employee of which company?

Answer: Motorola

Trivia Snapshot: The first mobile phone call was made on April 3, 1973, by Martin Cooper, an engineer and executive at Motorola. Cooper made the call on a prototype of what would become the Motorola DynaTAC, the world's first commercial handheld cellular phone. This historic call marked the beginning of the mobile telecommunications era, heralding a technological revolution that would lead to the ubiquitous use of mobile phones and fundamentally change the way people communicate.

Question: Which iconic product, launched by Apple in 1976, was one of the first successful personal computers?

Answer: Apple I

Trivia Snapshot: The Apple I, introduced by Apple Computer (now Apple Inc.) in 1976, was one of the first successful personal computers and marked the beginning of Apple's impact on the computing world. Designed and hand-built by Steve Wozniak, the Apple I was a breakthrough in terms of its user-friendly design and integration of a keyboard and monitor. Steve Jobs, Apple's co-founder, saw the commercial potential of Wozniak's creation, leading to the formation of the company and the beginning of a new era in personal computing.

Question: In what year was the first version of the programming language 'C' developed?

Answer: 1972

Trivia Snapshot: The programming language 'C' was developed in 1972 by Dennis Ritchie at Bell Labs. It was created for use with the Unix operating system, another landmark in computing developed at Bell Labs. 'C' is known for its efficiency and versatility and has had a profound influence on many other popular programming languages. Its development was a significant milestone in the field of computer science, laying the groundwork for the modern software development industry.

Question: Which spacecraft was launched in 1977 to study the outer planets and is still sending data back to Earth?

Answer: Voyager 1

Trivia Snapshot: Voyager 1, launched by NASA in 1977, is a space probe designed to study the outer Solar System and interstellar space. It has provided humanity with stunning images and data from Jupiter, Saturn, and their moons. Voyager 1 became the first human-made object to enter interstellar space in 2012. Its scientific discoveries and the messages of human culture it carries (on the Golden Record) make it one of the most significant and far-reaching missions in space exploration history. It continues to transmit valuable scientific data, expanding our understanding of the universe.

Question: What significant global environmental event was first celebrated on April 22, 1970?

Answer: Earth Day

Trivia Snapshot: Earth Day, first celebrated on April 22, 1970, was a watershed moment in the global environmental movement. Initiated in the United States by Senator Gaylord Nelson as an environmental teach-in, Earth Day drew public attention to environmental issues such as pollution, wildlife extinction, and deforestation. The event marked a significant shift in public awareness and led to the establishment of various environmental laws and policies. Earth Day has since grown into a global event celebrated by millions of people around the world, continuing to raise awareness and promote action for environmental protection.

Question: Which book by Rachel Carson, published earlier in 1962, is often credited with advancing the environmental movement?

Answer: Silent Spring

Trivia Snapshot: "Silent Spring," written by Rachel Carson and published in 1962, played a crucial role in the birth of the environmental movement. The book focused on the harmful effects of pesticides, particularly DDT, on wildlife and human ealth. Its compelling narrative raised awareness about environmental issues and led to a change in public perception about the use of chemicals. The impact of "Silent Spring" was significant, contributing to the eventual ban of DDT in the United States and inspiring an environmental consciousness that led to the establishment of the U.S. Environmental Protection Agency.

Question: In 1972, the United Nations held its first conference focused on human environmental issues in which city?

Answer: Stockholm

Trivia Snapshot: The 1972 United Nations Conference on the Human Environment, held in Stockholm, Sweden, was the first major international meeting focused on environmental issues. Known as the Stockholm Conference, it marked the beginning of a global dialogue on the interconnectedness of environment and development. The conference led to the establishment of the United Nations Environment Programme (UNEP) and laid the groundwork for future international environmental agreements and policies.

Question: What was the main focus of the 1973 Endangered Species Act in the United States?

Answer: Protecting threatened and endangered species

Trivia Snapshot: The Endangered Species Act of 1973 is a key piece of environmental legislation in the United States aimed at protecting species threatened with extinction. The Act provides a framework for the conservation and protection of endangered and threatened plants and animals and their habitats. It has been instrumental in saving numerous species from extinction and is considered one of the most comprehensive laws of its kind in the world.

Question: Which international agreement, signed in 1973, aimed to conserve endangered plants and animals?

Answer: CITES (Convention on International Trade in Endangered Species)

Trivia Snapshot: CITES (Convention on International Trade in Endangered Species of Wild Fauna and Flora), signed in 1973, is an international agreement between governments to ensure that the international trade in specimens of wild animals and plants does not threaten their survival. The convention plays a critical role in the conservation of biodiversity by regulating and monitoring the trade in endangered species. CITES is a key tool in the fight against wildlife trafficking and has been instrumental in the protection of various species around the world

Question: Who founded Greenpeace in 1971?

Answer: A group of activists in Vancouver, Canada

Trivia Snapshot: Greenpeace, one of the most recognized environmental organizations in the world, was founded in 1971 by a group of activists in Vancouver, Canada. The organization began as a small group protesting against U.S. nuclear testing at Amchitka Island in Alaska. Greenpeace quickly grew into an international movement focused on a wide range of environmental issues, including anti-whaling campaigns, deforestation, and climate change. Known for its direct-action tactics, Greenpeace has played a significant role in raising global environmental awareness and advocating for ecological preservation.

Question: What was the primary goal of the Clean Air Act, significantly amended in 1970?

Answer: To control air pollution on a national level

Trivia Snapshot: The Clean Air Act, significantly amended in 1970, is a landmark environmental law in the United States designed to control air pollution on a national level. The Act established comprehensive federal and state regulations to limit emissions from both stationary (industrial) sources and mobile sources. It authorized the Environmental Protection Agency (EPA) to set and enforce air quality standards and to regulate the emission of hazardous air pollutants. The Clean Air Act has been a key piece of environmental legislation in reducing air pollution and protecting public health in the United States.

Question: What environmental disaster occurred in 1979, leading to a significant nuclear accident?

Answer: Three Mile Island accident

Trivia Snapshot: The Three Mile Island accident was a significant nuclear power plant accident that occurred on March 28, 1979, near

Harrisburg, Pennsylvania. It was the most serious accident in U.S. commercial nuclear power plant history. The incident involved a partial meltdown of the reactor core but did not lead to a significant release of radiation to the environment. However, it had a profound impact on public perception of nuclear power and led to changes in nuclear regulatory and safety policies in the United States. The Three Mile Island accident is often cited in discussions about nuclear energy and its associated risks

Question: Which term, coined in the 1970s, refers to a proposed geological epoch recognizing human impact on Earth's ecosystems?

Answer: Anthropocene

Trivia Snapshot: The term "Anthropocene" was coined to describe a proposed new geological epoch that recognizes the significant impact of human activity on Earth's geology and ecosystems. The concept emerged as scientists began to notice that human actions – such as industrialization, nuclear tests, and massive changes to landscapes – were leaving a distinct mark on geological strata, akin to natural forces. While not officially recognized as a formal geological epoch, the term has gained widespread use in scientific and environmental discourse, highlighting the profound influence humans have on the planet.

Question: In 1979, which international treaty was signed to protect the ozone layer?

Answer: Vienna Convention for the Protection of the Ozone Layer

Trivia Snapshot: The Vienna Convention for the Protection of the Ozone Layer, signed in 1979, was a major international agreement aimed at protecting the Earth's ozone layer, which shields the planet from harmful ultraviolet radiation. The Convention established a framework for international cooperation in researching and monitoring ozone depletion and laid the groundwork for the Montreal Protocol, which was agreed upon in 1987 to phase out the production of numerous substances responsible for ozone depletion. The Vienna Convention was a significant step in global environmental policy, leading to successful efforts in reducing substances that harm the ozone layer.

Question: Which U.S. President resigned in 1974 due to the Watergate scandal?

Answer: Richard Nixon

Trivia Snapshot: Richard Nixon, the 37th President of the United States, resigned from office on August 8, 1974, due to the Watergate scandal. Nixon's resignation came after the revelation of his administration's involvement in a break-in at the Democratic National Committee headquarters at the Watergate office complex and subsequent attempts to cover up its involvement. Facing almost certain impeachment and removal from office, Nixon became the first U.S. president to resign. His resignation was a landmark moment in American politics and had a profound impact on the country's perception of political leadership and integrity.

Question: The Vietnam War ended in 1975 with the fall of which city?

Answer: Ho Chi Minh City (Saigon)

Trivia Snapshot: The Vietnam War ended in 1975 with the fall of Saigon, now known as Ho Chi Minh City, to the North Vietnamese forces. This event marked the capture of the largest city in South

Vietnam and the effective end of the war. The fall of Saigon led to the reunification of Vietnam under communist control and was a significant moment in 20th- century history. The images of the evacuation of American and South Vietnamese personnel and the broader implications of the war's end had a lasting impact on global politics and American foreign policy.

Question: Which country's revolution in 1979 led to the establishment of an Islamic Republic?

Answer: Iran

Trivia Snapshot: The Iranian Revolution of 1979 led to the overthrow of the Pahlavi dynasty under Shah Mohammad Reza Pahlavi and the establishment of an Islamic Republic under the leadership of Ayatollah Ruhollah Khomeini. The revolution was a pivotal event in Iran's history and significantly impacted global politics. It was marked by widespread demonstrations and civil unrest against the Shah's regime, driven by a combination of factors including political repression, economic hardship, and religious ideology. The establishment of the Islamic Republic marked a major shift in Iran's political and social landscape.

Question: What was the main purpose of the Camp David Accords signed in 1978?

Answer: To establish peace between Israel and Egypt

Trivia Snapshot: The Camp David Accords, signed in 1978, were a historic agreement brokered by U.S. President Jimmy Carter between Israeli Prime Minister Menachem Begin and Egyptian President Anwar Sadat. The accords led to the signing of the Egypt-Israel Peace Treaty in 1979. This agreement marked the first time an Arab country recognized

Israel and the first peace agreement between Israel and one of its Arab neighbors. The Accords were a significant step towards achieving peace in the Middle East, although they also led to controversy and opposition in the Arab world.

Question: In 1971, which country was divided into two, leading to the creation of Bangladesh?

Answer: Pakistan

Trivia Snapshot: In 1971, East Pakistan declared independence from West Pakistan, leading to the creation of the nation of Bangladesh. The Bangladesh Liberation War, which ensued, was marked by significant violence and humanitarian crisis.

The war ended with the victory of the Bangladeshi forces, supported by India, over Pakistan. The creation of Bangladesh was a significant event in South Asian history, reshaping the region's political and cultural landscape.

Question: Who became the first female Prime Minister of a major Western power in 1979?

Answer: Margaret Thatcher

Trivia Snapshot: Margaret Thatcher became the first female Prime Minister of the United Kingdom in 1979, making her the first woman to hold that office in a major Western power. Known as the "Iron Lady," Thatcher was a leader of the Conservative Party and served as Prime Minister until 1990. Her tenure was marked by significant economic and social reforms, a strong stance against the Soviet Union, and a controversial domestic policy that included privatization and deregulation. Thatcher's leadership and policies had a profound impact on British politics and global affairs.

Question: Which landmark U.S. Supreme Court decision in 1973 ruled that abortion rights fall within the privacy guaranteed by the 14th Amendment?

Answer: Roe v. Wade

Trivia Snapshot: Roe v. Wade was a landmark decision made by the U.S. Supreme Court in 1973. The Court ruled that the Constitution of the United States protects a pregnant woman's liberty to choose to have an abortion without excessive government restriction. This ruling was based on the right to privacy protected by the Due Process Clause of the 14th Amendment. Roe v. Wade remains one of the most debated and controversial court decisions in American history, significantly impacting U.S. reproductive laws and policies.

Question: The Munich massacre, involving the hostage-taking of Israeli Olympic team members, occurred during which Olympic Games?

Answer: 1972 Munich

Trivia Snapshot: The Munich massacre occurred during the 1972 Summer Olympics in Munich, Germany. Members of the Israeli Olympic team were taken hostage by the Palestinian terrorist group Black September. The tragic event ended with the death of 11 Israeli athletes and coaches and a West German police officer. The Munich massacre was a shocking incident that brought the Israeli-Palestinian conflict into the global spotlight and led to increased security measures at future Olympic Games.

Question: In 1972, President Richard Nixon made a historic visit to which country, significantly altering Cold War dynamics?

Answer: China

Trivia Snapshot: In 1972, U.S. President Richard Nixon made a historic visit to the People's Republic of China, marking the first time a U.S. president had visited the country since its founding in 1949. Nixon's visit initiated a process of

rapprochement between the United States and China, altering Cold War dynamics and leading to the eventual normalization of diplomatic relations. This significant event in international diplomacy opened up China to the Western world and shifted the balance of power during the Cold War.

Question: The first test-tube baby was born in 1978 in which country?

Answer: United Kingdom

Trivia Snapshot: The world's first test-tube baby, Louise Brown, was born in the United Kingdom in 1978. This momentous event marked the first successful birth of a child conceived through in vitro fertilization (IVF). The birth of Louise Brown represented a breakthrough in reproductive technology, offering hope to millions of infertile couples around the world. The success of IVF has since led to the birth of millions of babies and has had a profound impact on reproductive medicine and ethics.

Question: Which 1975 movie, directed by Steven Spielberg, is often credited as the first major summer blockbuster?

Answer: Jaws

Trivia Snapshot: "Jaws," directed by Steven Spielberg and released in 1975, is widely regarded as the first major summer blockbuster. The film's success created a new paradigm for the release and marketing of movies. "Jaws" captivated audiences with its thrilling story of a great white shark terrorizing a small beach town, and its impact on the film industry was profound. It set the stage for the modern blockbuster era, where high-action, high-budget films dominate the summer movie season.

Question: Who directed the 1972 crime film 'The Godfather'?

Answer: Francis Ford Coppola

Trivia Snapshot: "The Godfather," directed by Francis Ford Coppola and released in 1972, is one of the most acclaimed films in world cinema. Based on the novel by Mario Puzo, the film chronicles the powerful Italian-American crime family of Don Vito Corleone. Coppola's masterful storytelling, combined with stellar performances, transformed the film into a cinematic masterpiece. "The Godfather" won three Academy Awards, including Best Picture, and its influence on the film industry and popular culture is immense.

Question: Which science fiction film released in 1977 became a cultural phenomenon and spawned a major franchise?

Answer: Star Wars

Trivia Snapshot: "Star Wars," released in 1977 and later retitled "Star Wars: Episode IV – A New Hope," was a groundbreaking science fiction film directed by George Lucas. The film was a massive success, captivating audiences with its innovative special effects, engaging storyline, and memorable characters. It not only became a cultural phenomenon but also spawned a major franchise, including sequels, prequels, television series, books, and more. "Star Wars" has had a significant impact on popular culture and the film industry, inspiring generations of filmmakers and fans.

Question: What was the name of the first African American to win an Academy Award for Best Actor, which he received in 1964 for 'Lilies of the Field'?

Answer: Sidney Poitier

Trivia Snapshot: Sidney Poitier made history in 1964 when he became the first African American to win an Academy Award for Best Actor for his role in "Lilies of the Field." In the film, Poitier played Homer Smith, a traveling handyman who helps a group of German-speaking nuns build a chapel. His groundbreaking win was a significant milestone in the history of cinema, paving the way for future generations of African American actors and actresses in Hollywood. Poitier's distinguished career and pioneering achievements have made him an iconic figure in the film industry.

Question: Which 1976 movie featured Robert De Niro's famous line, "You talkin' to me?"

Answer: Taxi Driver

Trivia Snapshot: "Taxi Driver," released in 1976 and directed by Martin Scorsese, is a psychological thriller featuring Robert De Niro as Travis Bickle. De Niro's character, a mentally unstable Vietnam War veteran and taxi driver in New York City, delivers the famous line, "You talkin' to me?" during a monologue in front of a mirror. This line has become one of the most iconic in film history, reflecting the character's growing alienation and aggression. "Taxi Driver" is widely regarded as a cinematic masterpiece and a landmark film in the psychological thriller genre.

Question: The 1970s saw the rise of martial arts films. Which actor became synonymous with this genre?

Answer: Bruce Lee

Trivia Snapshot: Bruce Lee is arguably the most influential martial artist of the 20th century and became synonymous with the martial arts film genre in the 1970s. His films, including "Enter the Dragon," "The Way of the Dragon," and "Fist of Fury," showcased his exceptional martial arts skills and charismatic screen presence. Lee's impact on martial arts and popular culture extends beyond his films; he was also a philosopher and the founder of Jeet Kune Do. Bruce Lee's legacy in martial arts cinema and his contribution to changing perceptions of Asians in American films are profound. Question: What film won the Academy Award for Best Picture in 1979?

Answer: Kramer vs. Kramer

Trivia Snapshot: "Kramer vs. Kramer," a drama film released in 1979, won the Academy Award for Best Picture. Directed by Robert Benton and starring Dustin Hoffman and Meryl Streep, the film explores the emotional and legal struggles of a couple going through a divorce and the ensuing custody battle over their son. The film was praised for its powerful performances and its sensitive portrayal of changing family dynamics and gender roles. "Kramer vs. Kramer" was a critical and commercial success, winning several Oscars, including Best Director, Best Actor for Hoffman, and Best Supporting Actress for Streep.

Question: Which movie musical set in the 1950s and starring John Travolta and Olivia Newton-John became a huge hit in 1978?

Answer: Grease

Trivia Snapshot: "Grease," released in 1978, is a musical romantic comedy set in the 1950s, starring John Travolta as Danny Zuko and Olivia Newton-John as Sandy Olsson. The film, based on the 1971 musical of the same name, became a massive box office success and a cultural phenomenon. Its portrayal of teenage love, high school life, and 1950s nostalgia, combined with catchy songs and energetic dance numbers, made it one of the most popular usicals of all time. The soundtrack of "Grease," featuring hits like "You're the One That I Want" and "Summer Nights," has enjoyed enduring popularity.

Question: Which horror film, directed by William Friedkin in 1973, became one of the most profitable horror movies ever made?

Answer: The Exorcist

Trivia Snapshot: "The Exorcist," is widely regarded as one of the greatest and most profitable horror films ever made. Based on the 1971 novel of the same name by William Peter Blatty, the film revolves around the demonic possession of a young girl and her mother's desperate attempts to save her through anexorcism conducted by two priests. "The Exorcist" was notable for its disturbing content, innovative special effects, and powerful performances.

Question: In the 1979 film 'Alien,' who played the character of Ellen Ripley?

Answer: Sigourney Weaver

1980s

The MTV Generation

1980s

Story Time

The Arcade Championship of 1983

In the bustling summer of 1983, the small town of Oakridge was about to witness an event that would go down in its history. The local arcade, 'Pixel Palace,' announced the first-ever 'Oakridge Arcade Championship,' sparking excitement among the town's youth and nostalgic adults alike. The game of choice? The iconic 'Pac-Man.'

Word spread quickly, and the competition drew participants of all ages. There was Billy, the high school's video game wizard; Susan, a middle-aged librarian with a surprising knack for arcade games; and Mr. Thompson, the retired veteran who hadn't touched a game since pinball in the '50s.

The arcade was decked out with neon lights and posters of 80s pop icons. On the day of the championship, Pixel Palace was packed to the rafters. The local radio station set up a booth outside, and the air was electric with excitement and the distinct blips and bleeps of arcade games.

As the competition commenced, it was clear this was more than just a game. It was a battle of focus, agility, and quick thinking. Billy breezed through the early rounds, while Susan's methodical approach surprised many as she racked up high scores. Mr. Thompson, cheered on by a growing fanbase, discovered his pinball skills translated surprisingly well to the world of Pac-Man.

The final round was a showdown between Billy and Susan, the teenager versus the librarian. The crowd was on the edge of their seats as they navigated Pac-Man through the maze, gobbling up dots and avoiding ghosts. In a stunning upset,

Susan clinched the victory in the last seconds with a risky move that paid off.

The Arcade Championship of 1983 became more than just a competition; it was a celebration of a community coming together, bridging generational gaps, and finding joy in the shared language of video games. Susan became a local hero, her photo proudly displayed at Pixel Palace, and the story of her victory was talked about for years to come. It was a reminder that in Oakridge, fun and camaraderie were always just a quarter away.

Did you know that Pac-Man, the iconic arcade game released in 1980, holds the Guinness World Record for the most successful coin-operated arcade game ever? Created by Japanese designer Toru Iwatani, Pac-Man became a cultural phenomenon, inspiring merchandise, spin-off games, a television series, and even a hit single. With its simple yet addictive gameplay and memorable characters, Pac-Man remains a beloved classic in the world of video games, transcending generations and continuing to captivate players worldwide.

Memory Lane

1980s Cultural Highlights

MTV and the Music Video Revolution:

The 1980s marked the dawn of the music video era, epitomized by the launch of MTV in 1981. This channel didn't just play music; it transformed the way music was consumed and appreciated. Iconic music videos like Michael Jackson's "Thriller" and Madonna's "Like a Virgin" became cultural landmarks. MTV was more than a channel; it was a window to a new world of music, fashion, and pop culture.

Rise of Blockbuster Sequels and Action Heroes:

Cinema in the 1980s was dominated by action heroes and blockbuster sequels. Movies like

"The Terminator," "Die Hard," and the "Indiana Jones" series captivated audiences with their mix

of adrenaline-pumping action and charismatic leads. These films weren't just box office hits; they were a part of the decade's cultural fabric, giving rise to iconic characters and unforgettable catchphrases.

The Personal Computer Revolution:

The 1980s witnessed the personal computer becoming a household item, fundamentally changing how people worked, played, and communicated. The introduction of the Apple Macintosh, IBM PC, and Microsoft Windows signaled a new era in technology. These advancements weren't just about processing power; they represented a shift towards a future where computers would be an integral part of daily life.

Fashion: Bold Colors and New Wave Style:

Fashion in the 1980s was characterized by bold colors, big hair, and the rise of new wave style. From the power suits with shoulder pads to the aerobics craze led by Jane Fonda, the fashion was as vibrant and diverse as the decade itself. It was a time when style was not just about clothing; it was a statement of identity and freedom of expression.

The Golden Age of Video Games:

The 1980s was also the golden age of arcade video games. Classics like "Pac-Man," "Space Invaders," and "Donkey Kong" not only dominated arcades but also entered homes with the advent of gaming consoles like the Nintendo Entertainment System. These games weren't just pastimes; they were a significant part of youth culture and a precursor to the digital entertainment revolution.

Did you know that Donkey Kong, the classic arcade game released by Nintendo in 1981, marked the debut of two iconic video game characters: Mario (originally known as Jumpman) and Donkey Kong himself? Created by legendary game designer Shigeru Miyamoto, Donkey Kong was one of the earliest platform games, challenging players to rescue a damsel in distress from the clutches of the giant ape Donkey Kong. Despite its simplistic graphics and gameplay, Donkey Kong's innovative design and challenging levels paved the way for the success of Nintendo and established Mario as one of the most recognizable characters in gaming history.

Quiz Time

Which cable channel, launched in 1981, revolutionized music by airing music videos 24/7?

- VH1
- MTV
- YT Music

Which 1983 music video by Michael Jackson is famed for its elaborate dance sequences and special effects?

- Beat It
- Thriller
- Billie Jean

Madonna first reached the top of the Billboard charts in 1984 with which song?

- Like a Virgin
- Material
- Girl Holiday

The 1985 charity song "We Are the World" was recorded by a group of famous musicians collectively known as what?

- Band Aid
- USA for Africa
- Live Aid

Which iconic 1980s movie featured a time-traveling DeLorean car?

- Blade Runner
- Back to the Future
- The Terminator

Who became a pop icon and sex symbol after her role in the 1981 film 'The Blue Lagoon'?

- Brooke Shields
- Molly Ringwald
- Demi Moore

Did you know that the original "Blade Runner" initially received mixed reviews from critics and struggled at the box office? Despite its initial commercial disappointment, the film gained a cult following.

In 1989, which sitcom about a group of friends living in New York City debuted

- Friends
- Seinfeld
- Cheers

What was the best-selling album of the 1980s, released by Michael Jackson in 1982?

- Bad
- Thriller
- Off the Wall

Which iconic 1980s action movie coined the catchphrase "I'll be back"?

- Die Hard
- Rambo
- The Terminator

Did you know that Die Hard was originally based on the novel "Nothing Lasts Forever" by Roderick Thorp, which itself was a sequel to the novel "The Detective"? The film follows New York City cop John McClane, played by Bruce Willis

In what year was the first IBM personal computer released?

- 1981
- 1984
- 986

Which 1980s video game, featuring falling block puzzles, became one of the best-selling video games of all time?

- Super Mario Bros.
- Pac-Man
- Tetris

Who is credited with inventing the World Wide Web in 1989?

- Tim Berners-Lee
- Bill Gates
- Steve Jobs

Did you know that the iconic film "Top Gun," was originally inspired by a magazine article titled "Top Guns" published in California Magazine? The article highlighted the experiences of U.S. Navy fighter pilots, which eventually led to the development of the blockbuster film.

Which iconic 1980s toy allowed users to create glowing designs using small colored pegs?

- Lite-Brite
- Rubik's Cube
- Simon

Apple Inc. released its first Macintosh computer in what year?

- 1980
- 1984
- 1986

What was the name of the first commercially successful graphical user interface-based operating system, released by Microsoft in 1985?

- MS-DOS
- Windows 1.0
- Mac OS

Did you know that the iconic Macintosh commercial was directed by Ridley Scott? This advertisement, which aired during the Super Bowl, is considered one of the greatest commercials of all time and marked a significant moment in the history of personal computing.

Which portable gaming console, released by Nintendo in 1989, became an instant hit worldwide?

- Game Boy
- Sega Genesis
- Atari Lynx

In 1983, which technology, allowing mobile phones to connect over long distances, was first introduced?

- The Internet
- Cellular Networks
- Satellite Communications

The first version of which digital image editing software was released in 1988?

- Adobe Photoshop
- Microsoft Paint
- CorelDRAW

Did you know that the original Game Boy was almost named the "Game Boy Kidd" in honor of its creator, Gunpei Yokoi? However, Yokoi preferred a simpler and more universal name.

Which iconic 1980s arcade game featured a character eating dots and being chased by ghosts in a maze?

- Space Invaders
- Pac-Man
- Donkey Kong

Which event in 1989 symbolized the end of the Cold War and the division of East and West Germany?

- The signing of the Treaty of Versailles
- The fall of a wall
- The death of Stalin

What was the primary focus of Mikhail Gorbachev's policies of Glasnost and Perestroika in the Soviet Union during the late 1980s?

- Economic reform and openness
- Military expansion
- Nuclear disarmament

Did you know that during the Cold War, East Germany had its own currency called the "East German Mark"

Which two countries signed the Intermediate-Range Nuclear Forces Treaty in 1987?

- United States and Soviet Union

- United States and China

- Soviet Union and United Kingdom

The Tiananmen Square protests, a major pro-democracy movement, occurred in 1989 in which country?

- China

- Japan

- South Korea

In 1983, the United States invaded which Caribbean island, marking a significant event in Cold War politics?

- Cuba

- Grenada

- Jamaica

Did you know that Grenada has a rich history and culture, including being known as the "Spice Isle" due to its production of nutmeg and other spices. Additionally, Grenada is famous for its stunning beaches, lush rainforests, and vibrant local cuisine.

Who was elected as President of South Africa in 1989 and played a crucial role in ending apartheid?

- Nelson Mandela

- F.W. de Klerk

- Desmond Tutu

Which Middle Eastern conflict began in 1980 and lasted for eight years?

- The Gulf War

- The Arab-Israeli War

- The Iran-Iraq War

In 1982, which conflict occurred between the United Kingdom and Argentina?

- The Falklands War

- The Gulf War

- The Suez Crisis

Did you know that the Suez Canal remains one of the world's most vital waterways, Spanning approximately 120 miles (193 kilometers) across Egypt, the canal facilitates the passage of over 10% of global maritime trade

Who became the first woman to be appointed to the Supreme Court of the United States in 1981?

- Ruth Bader Ginsburg
- Sandra Day O'Connor
- Sonia Sotomayor

What fashion trend, involving brightly colored clothing and accessories, was popular in the 1980s?

- Grunge style
- Neon colors
- Hippie style

Which hairstyle, characterized by volume and height, became iconic of the 1980s?

- The Bob
- The Mullet
- Big hair

Did you know that Ruth Bader Ginsburg was the first female tenured professor at Columbia Law School and co-founded the Women's Rights Project at the American Civil Liberties Union (ACLU).

Which fitness trend, popularized by celebrities like Jane Fonda, led to the widespread use of leotards and headbands in the 1980s?

- Yoga

- Aerobics

- Pilates

Did you know during the 1980s, Asia underwent a profound economic transformation, propelling several countries in the region to global prominence. Japan solidified its position as the world's second-largest economy, driven by the success of iconic companies like Sony and Toyota. South Korea's "Miracle on the Han River" saw rapid industrialization and democratization, with chaebols like Samsung and Hyundai leading the charge. Taiwan and Singapore also experienced impressive growth, becoming manufacturing and financial hubs, respectively. Collectively known as the "Four Asian Tigers," these nations laid the groundwork for Asia's continued economic ascent in the 21st century

What iconic item of clothing was popularized by the film 'Flashdance' and became a fashion trend in the 1980s?

- Shoulder pads

- Acid-wash jeans

- Off-the-shoulder sweatshirts

Which 1980s television show had a significant impact on men's fashion, particularly with pastel-colored suits and loafers?

- Miami Vice

- The A-Team

- Magnum P.I

What type of jeans, characterized by a stone-washed and distressed look, became fashionable in the 1980s?

- Skinny jeans

- Bell-bottoms

- Acid-wash jeans

Did you know that in the original "A-Team" TV series, the iconic black van used by the team was actually painted gray for the first season

Ray-Ban sunglasses gained immense popularity in the 1980s, partly due to their appearance in which hit movie?

- Top Gun

- Risky Business

- The Blues Brothers

The 'power suit,' often featuring shoulder pads and a tailored look, became a symbol of what in the 1980s?

- Casual style

- Women's empowerment in the workplace

- Teen fashion

Which type of shoe, characterized by thick soles and bold colors, became a must-have among teenagers in the 1980s?

- High-top sneakers

- Platform shoes

- Penny loafers

Did you know that "The Blues Brothers" was originally created as a musical sketch on "Saturday Night Live".

Which U.S. ice hockey team won the gold medal at the 1980 Winter Olympics, an event known as the 'Miracle on Ice'?

- The Detroit Red Wings

- The U.S. National Team

- The Chicago Blackhawks

Who set the men's 100m world record at the 1988 Seoul Olympics, only to be disqualified for doping?

- Carl Lewis
- Usain Bolt
- Ben Johnson

In 1984, which gymnast became the first to score a perfect 10 at the Olympics?

- Nadia Comăneci
- Mary Lou Retton
- Olga Korbut

Did you know that in the 1980s, Chicago, often referred to as the "Windy City," experienced a cultural and economic resurgence, marked by the revitalization of its downtown area and the emergence of influential artists in various fields such as music, theater, and visual arts.

Which NFL team won four Super Bowls in the 1980s, led by coach Bill Walsh and quarterback Joe Montana?

- Dallas Cowboys
- San Francisco 49ers
- Pittsburgh Steelers

Who won the Wimbledon Ladies' Singles title a record nine times between 1982 and 1990?

- Martina Navratilova
- Chris Evert
- Steffi Graf

In 1985, which 17-year-old became the youngest-ever male Grand Slam singles champion by winning the French Open?

- Andre Agassi
- Pete Sampras
- Michael Chang

Which basketball player, nicknamed 'Air', was drafted third overall by the Chicago Bulls in 1984?

- Magic Johnson
- Larry Bird
- Michael Jordan

Did you know that during the 1980s, the Soviet Union faced allegations of state-sponsored doping programs in various sports, particularly in Olympic competitions? Athletes from the Soviet Union were suspected of using performance-enhancing drugs to gain a competitive edge, leading to controversies and tarnishing the country's reputation in international sports.

What major sporting event did the Soviet Union boycott in 1984?

- The FIFA World Cup
- The Summer Olympics in Los Angeles
- The Winter Olympics in Sarajevo

Which famous boxer, known as 'The Hitman', won world titles in five different weight divisions in the 1980s?

- Mike Tyson
- Thomas Hearns
- Sugar Ray Leonard
- Tyson Fury

Did you know that outside of the boxing ring, Sugar Ray Leonard has been an advocate for various philanthropic causes? He has been involved in initiatives supporting diabetes research, anti-drug campaigns, and programs aimed at empowering youth through sports and education.

In 1980, which English football club began a dominant period, winning their first European Cup and six First Division titles during the decade?

- Manchester United

- Liverpool F.C.

- Arsenal F.C.

- Manchester City

Did you know that Everton Football Club, based in Liverpool, experienced a resurgence during the 1980s under the management of Howard Kendall? The team won the English First Division title in 1985 and 1987, as well as the FA Cup in 1984, cementing their status as one of the top clubs in English football during that era.

Did you know that during the 1980s, the Dallas Cowboys, led by legendary coach Tom Landry and quarterback Troy Aikman, continued their tradition of success, making multiple playoff appearances and winning Super Bowl titles in 1978 and 1993? The team remained one of the most iconic franchises in the NFL, known for their star-studded lineup and innovative strategies on the field.

Answers for Trivia 1980s

Question: Which cable channel, launched in 1981, revolutionized music by airing music videos 24/7?

Answer: MTV

Trivia Snapshot: MTV, or Music Television, was launched in 1981 and quickly became a cultural phenomenon, changing the way people consumed music. By airing music videos around the clock, MTV provided a platform for artists to showcase their work visually and contributed to the rise of music video as an art form.

Question: Which 1983 music video by Michael Jackson is famed for its elaborate dance sequences and special effects?

Answer: Thriller

Trivia Snapshot: Michael Jackson's "Thriller," released in 1983, is one of the most iconic music videos of all time. Directed by John Landis, the video features Jackson's intricate dance moves, groundbreaking special effects, and a memorable storyline, making it a cultural milestone in the history of music videos.

Question: Madonna first reached the top of the Billboard charts in 1984 with which song?

Answer: Like a Virgin

Trivia Snapshot: Madonna's "Like a Virgin," released in 1984, marked her first number-one hit on the Billboard Hot 100 chart. The song's provocative lyrics and catchy melody catapulted Madonna to superstardom and solidified her status as a pop icon of the 1980s.

Question: The 1985 charity song "We Are the World" was recorded by a group of famous musicians collectively known as what?

Answer: USA for Africa

Trivia Snapshot: "We Are the World," recorded in 1985, was a charity single written by Michael Jackson and Lionel Richie. The song featured an ensemble of renowned artists, including Stevie Wonder, Bruce Springsteen, and Diana Ross, who came together under the banner of USA for Africa to raise funds for famine relief in Africa.

Question: Which iconic 1980s movie featured a time-traveling DeLorean car?

Answer: Back to the Future

Trivia Snapshot: "Back to the Future," released in 1985 and directed by Robert Zemeckis, follows the adventures of Marty McFly, who travels back in time using a DeLorean car invented by his eccentric friend Doc Brown. The film became a beloved classic, known for its inventive storytelling and memorable characters.

Question: Who became a pop icon and sex symbol after her role in the 1981 film 'The Blue Lagoon'?

Answer: Brooke Shields

Trivia Snapshot: Brooke Shields gained widespread fame and recognition for her role in "The Blue Lagoon," released in 1981. The film, which depicted the romantic adventures of two young castaways, propelled Shields to stardom and solidified her status as a sex symbol of the 1980s.

Question: In 1989, which sitcom about a group of friends living in New York City debuted?

Answer: Friends

Trivia Snapshot: "Friends," created by David Crane and Marta Kauffman, premiered in 1989 and became one of the most popular and enduring sitcoms of all time. Set in New York City, the show followed the lives and relationships of six friends—Rachel, Ross, Monica, Chandler, Joey, and Phoebe—and resonated with audiences worldwide.

Question: What was the best-selling album of the 1980s, released by Michael Jackson in 1982?

Answer: Thriller

Trivia Snapshot: Michael Jackson's "Thriller," released in 1982, is widely regarded as the best-selling album of all time. Featuring hit singles like "Billie Jean" and "Beat It," along with the iconic title track, "Thriller" revolutionized the music industry and solidified Jackson's status as the King of Pop.

Question: Which iconic 1980s action movie coined the catchphrase "I'll be back"?

Answer: The Terminator

Trivia Snapshot: "The Terminator," released in 1984 and directed by James Cameron, introduced audiences to Arnold Schwarzenegger's iconic portrayal of the cyborg assassin known as the Terminator. The film's memorable catchphrase, "I'll be back," became synonymous with Schwarzenegger's character and has since become a pop culture staple.

Question: In what year was the first IBM personal computer released?

Answer: 1981

Trivia Snapshot: The first IBM personal computer, known as the IBM PC, was introduced in 1981. Developed by IBM, the PC revolutionized the personal computing industry and set the standard for future computer designs.

Question: Which 1980s video game, featuring falling block puzzles, became one of the best-selling video games of all time?

Answer: Tetris

Trivia Snapshot: "Tetris," created by Russian game designer Alexey Pajitnov in 1984, became one of the most popular and enduring video games of all time. Its simple yet addictive gameplay, involving arranging falling blocks to create complete lines, captivated players around the world and contributed to the widespread success of the game.

Question: Who is credited with inventing the World Wide Web in 1989?

Answer: Tim Berners-Lee

Trivia Snapshot: Tim Berners-Lee, a British computer scientist, is credited with inventing the World Wide Web in 1989 while working at CERN, the European Organization for Nuclear Research. Berners-Lee's creation revolutionized the way information is shared and accessed on the internet, laying the foundation for the modern digital age.

Question: Which iconic 1980s toy allowed users to create glowing designs using small colored pegs?

Answer: Lite-Brite

Trivia Snapshot: Lite-Brite, introduced by Hasbro in 1967 and popularized in the 1980s, allowed users to create glowing designs by inserting small colored pegs into a backlit board. The toy sparked creativity and imagination in children and became a beloved classic of the 1980s toy market.

Question: Apple Inc. released its first Macintosh computer in what year?

Answer: 1984

Trivia Snapshot: Apple Inc. released its first Macintosh computer, the Macintosh 128K, in 1984. Marketed as the first personal computer to feature a graphical user interface, the Macintosh revolutionized the computer industry and laid the groundwork for future innovations in computing technology.

Question: What was the name of the first commercially successful graphical user interface-based operating system, released by Microsoft in 1985?

Answer: Windows 1.0

Trivia Snapshot: Windows 1.0, released by Microsoft in 1985, was the company's first commercially successful graphical user interface-based operating system. It introduced features like overlapping windows, icons, and menus, setting the stage for Microsoft's dominance in the personal computer operating system market.

Question: Which portable gaming console, released by Nintendo in 1989, became an instant hit worldwide?

Answer: Game Boy

Trivia Snapshot: The Game Boy, released by Nintendo in 1989, became an instant hit worldwide and revolutionized the handheld gaming market. With its compact design, long battery life, and library of iconic games like "Tetris" and "Super Mario Land," the Game Boy became one of the most successful and enduring gaming platforms of all time.

Question: In 1983, which technology, allowing mobile phones to connect over long distances, was first introduced?

Answer: Satellite Communications

Trivia Snapshot: In 1983, satellite communications technology was first introduced, enabling mobile phones to connect over long distances via satellite signals. This technology expanded the reach of mobile telecommunications and paved the way for the development of modern satellite-based communication systems.

Question: The first version of which digital image editing software was released in 1988?

Answer: Adobe Photoshop

Trivia Snapshot: Adobe Photoshop, first released in 1988 by Adobe Inc., revolutionized digital image editing and became the industry standard for professional graphic design and photography. Its powerful features and intuitive interface have made it the go-to software for creative professionals worldwide.

Question: Which iconic 1980s arcade game featured a character eating dots and being chased by ghosts in a maze?

Answer: Pac-Man

Trivia Snapshot: Pac-Man, released by Namco in 1980, is one of the most iconic and influential arcade games of all time. Players control the titular character, Pac-Man, as he navigates mazes, eats dots, and avoids colorful ghosts. Pac-Man's simple yet addictive gameplay and charming characters have made it a timeless classic in the world of video games.

Question: Which event in 1989 symbolized the end of the Cold War and the division of East and West Germany?

Answer: The fall of a wall

Trivia Snapshot: The fall of the Berlin Wall in 1989 symbolized the end of the Cold War and the division between East and West Germany. The dismantling of this physical barrier, which had separated East Berlin from West Berlin since 1961, marked a significant moment in history and paved the way for German reunification.

Question: What was the primary focus of Mikhail Gorbachev's policies of Glasnost and Perestroika in the Soviet Union during the late 1980s?

Answer: Economic reform and openness

Trivia Snapshot: Mikhail Gorbachev's policies of Glasnost (openness) and Perestroika (restructuring) aimed to reform the Soviet Union's political and economic systems during the late 1980s. Glasnost promoted greater transparency and freedom of speech, while Perestroika focused on restructuring the economy to improve efficiency and productivity.

Question: Who became the first woman to be appointed to the Supreme Court of the United States in 1981?

Answer: Sandra Day O'Connor

Trivia Snapshot: Sandra Day O'Connor made history in 1981 when she became the first woman appointed to the Supreme Court of the United States. Serving as an Associate Justice until her retirement in 2006, O'Connor played a crucial role in shaping American jurisprudence and was known for her pragmatic approach to legal issues.

Question: What fashion trend, involving brightly colored clothing and accessories, was popular in the 1980s?

Answer: Neon colors

Trivia Snapshot: Neon colors, characterized by their vibrant and fluorescent hues, were a popular fashion trend in the 1980s. From neon pink leg warmers to electric blue eyeshadow, bright and bold colors dominated the fashion scene, reflecting the energetic and flamboyant spirit of the decade.

Question: Which hairstyle, characterized by volume and height, became iconic of the 1980s?

Answer: Big hair

Trivia Snapshot: Big hair, characterized by its volume, height, and often teased or permed texture, became an iconic hairstyle of the 1980s. Popularized by celebrities like Madonna and rock bands such as Bon Jovi, big hair epitomized the glamorous and over-the-top aesthetic of the decade's fashion and culture.

Question: Which fitness trend, popularized by celebrities like Jane Fonda, led to the widespread use of leotards and headbands in the 1980s?

Answer: Aerobics

Trivia Snapshot: Aerobics, a high-energy exercise routine that combines rhythmic aerobic movements with stretching and strength training, gained immense popularity in the 1980s. Fueled by the rise of fitness culture and iconic figures like Jane Fonda, aerobics classes became a staple in gyms and community centers across the globe. The trend was characterized by vibrant leotards, leg warmers, and headbands, as enthusiasts embraced the colorful and dynamic aesthetic of the era.

Question: What iconic item of clothing was popularized by the film 'Flashdance' and became a fashion trend in the 1980s?

Answer: Off-the-shoulder sweatshirts

Trivia Snapshot: The 1983 film 'Flashdance' popularized the trend of wearing off-the-shoulder sweatshirts, which became a fashion staple of the 1980s. Inspired by the film's protagonist, aspiring dancer Alex Owens, many young women embraced the casual yet stylish look of oversized sweatshirts worn off one shoulder. This fashion trend symbolized the era's emphasis on individuality and self-expression, reflecting the spirit of youth culture in the 1980s.

Question: Which 1980s television show had a significant impact on men's fashion, particularly with pastel-colored suits and loafers?

Answer: Miami Vice

Trivia Snapshot: "Miami Vice," a popular television series that aired from 1984 to 1989, revolutionized men's fashion with its sleek and sophisticated aesthetic. The show's protagonists, Detectives Sonny Crockett and Ricardo Tubbs, portrayed by Don Johnson and Philip Michael Thomas, became style icons known for their pastel-colored suits, T-shirts, and loafers—setting new trends in menswear. The fashion influence of "Miami Vice" extended beyond the small screen, shaping the wardrobes of men worldwide and epitomizing the chic, urban look of the 1980s.

Question: What type of jeans, characterized by a stone-washed and distressed look, became fashionable in the 1980s?

Answer: Acid-wash jeans

Trivia Snapshot: Acid-wash jeans, characterized by their distinctive bleached or "acid-washed" appearance and often featuring frayed edges or holes, became a fashion phenomenon in the 1980s. The unique texture and vintage appeal of acid-wash denim appealed to the era's youthful and rebellious spirit, making them a staple of casual wear. From celebrities to streetwear enthusiasts, acid-wash jeans were embraced as a symbol of individuality and edgy style during the vibrant fashion era of the 1980s.

Question: Ray-Ban sunglasses gained immense popularity in the 1980s, partly due to their appearance in which hit movie?

Answer: Top Gun

Trivia Snapshot: Ray-Ban sunglasses experienced a surge in popularity during the 1980s, thanks in part to their prominent appearance in the blockbuster film "Top Gun," released in 1986. The film's protagonist, Maverick, played by Tom Cruise, famously wore Ray-Ban Aviator sunglasses throughout the movie, propelling the brand to new heights of coolness and style. As a result, Ray-Ban Aviators became a must-have accessory for fans of the film and fashion-conscious individuals alike, solidifying their status as an iconic symbol of 1980s pop culture.

Question: The 'power suit,' often featuring shoulder pads and a tailored look, became a symbol of what in the 1980s?

Answer: Women's empowerment in the workplace

Trivia Snapshot: The 'power suit,' characterized by its structured silhouette, padded shoulders, and tailored fit, emerged as a symbol of women's empowerment in the workplace during the 1980s. As more women entered corporate environments and sought to break through the glass ceiling, the power suit became a sartorial expression of their ambition, confidence, and professionalism. Worn by influential figures like business executives and political leaders, the power suit represented a shift towards gender equality and challenged traditional notions of femininity in the professional world.

Question: Which type of shoe, characterized by thick soles and bold colors, became a must-have among teenagers in the 1980s?

Answer: High-top sneakers

Trivia Snapshot: High-top sneakers, distinguished by their extended ankle collar and thick rubber soles, became a fashion must-have among teenagers in the 1980s. Popularized by athletes, musicians, and celebrities, high-tops epitomized the era's casual and athletic style. Brands like Nike, Adidas, and Converse offered a wide range of high-top sneaker designs, often featuring bold colors, contrasting panels, and eye-catching patterns. Whether on the basketball court or the city streets, high-top sneakers were a staple footwear choice for the youth culture of the 1980s, embodying a sense of rebellion, individuality, and urban cool.

Question: Which U.S. ice hockey team won the gold medal at the 1980 Winter Olympics, an event known as the 'Miracle on Ice'?

Answer: The U.S. National Team

Trivia Snapshot: The U.S. National Team, composed of amateur and collegiate players, achieved a historic victory at the 1980 Winter Olympics in Lake Placid, New York, by winning the gold medal in men's ice hockey. Their triumph, known as the 'Miracle on Ice,' stunned the world as they defeated the heavily favored Soviet Union team in a thrilling semifinal match. Coached by Herb Brooks, the young American squad's improbable journey to gold captivated the nation and remains one of the most memorable moments in Olympic history.

Question: Who set the men's 100m world record at the 1988 Seoul Olympics, only to be disqualified for doping?

Answer: Ben Johnson

Trivia Snapshot: Ben Johnson, a Canadian sprinter, set a new world record in the men's 100m dash at the 1988 Summer Olympics in Seoul, South Korea, with a time of 9.79 seconds. However, Johnson's triumph was short-lived as he was subsequently disqualified after testing positive for anabolic steroids. His doping scandal shocked the world and raised questions about the integrity of athletics, leading to increased scrutiny and anti-doping measures in sports. Johnson's downfall served as a cautionary tale about the consequences of cheating and the importance of fair competition in the Olympic Games.

Question: In 1984, which gymnast became the first to score a perfect 10 at the Olympics?

Answer: Mary Lou Retton

Trivia Snapshot: Mary Lou Retton, an American gymnast, made history at the 1984 Summer Olympics in Los Angeles by becoming the first female gymnast to score a perfect 10 in the Olympic Games. Her flawless performance on the vault during the all-around competition propelled her to victory, earning her the gold medal and cementing her status as an American sports icon. Retton's electrifying display of athleticism and determination captivated audiences worldwide, inspiring a new generation of gymnasts and leaving an indelible mark on Olympic history.

Question: Which NFL team won four Super Bowls in the 1980s, led by coach Bill Walsh and quarterback Joe Montana?

Answer: San Francisco 49ers

Trivia Snapshot: The San Francisco 49ers dominated the NFL in the 1980s, winning four Super Bowl championships under the leadership of head coach Bill Walsh and star quarterback Joe Montana. Known for their innovative West Coast offense and stellar defense, the 49ers became a powerhouse in professional football, capturing titles in Super Bowls XVI (1982), XIX (1985), XXIII (1989), and XXIV (1990). With a roster featuring legendary players like Jerry Rice, Ronnie Lott, and Dwight Clark, the 49ers' success during the decade solidified their status as one of the greatest dynasties in NFL history.

Question: Who won the Wimbledon Ladies' Singles title a record nine times between 1982 and 1990?

Answer: Martina Navratilova

Trivia Snapshot: Martina Navratilova, one of the greatest tennis players of all time, dominated the Wimbledon Ladies' Singles competition in the 1980s, winning a record nine titles between 1982 and 1990. Known for her powerful serve-and-volley style and remarkable athleticism, Navratilova's dominance on grass courts made her virtually unbeatable at the All England Club. Her unparalleled success at Wimbledon solidified her status as a tennis icon and earned her a place among the sport's legends.

Question: In 1985, which 17-year-old became the youngest-ever male Grand Slam singles champion by winning the French Open?

Answer: Michael Chang

Trivia Snapshot: Michael Chang, a rising tennis star from the United States, made history at the 1989 French Open by becoming the youngest-ever male Grand Slam singles champion at the age of 17. Known for his speed, agility, and tenacity on the court, Chang's unexpected victory over top-seeded Ivan Lendl in the fourth round propelled him to the title, marking a watershed moment in tennis history. Chang's remarkable achievement at Roland Garros catapulted him to international fame and inspired a new generation of young tennis players around the world.

Question: Which basketball player, nicknamed 'Air', was drafted third overall by the Chicago Bulls in 1984?

Answer: Michael Jordan

Trivia Snapshot: Michael Jordan, widely regarded as the greatest basketball player of all time, was drafted by the Chicago Bulls with the third overall pick in the 1984 NBA Draft. Known for his extraordinary athleticism, unparalleled skill, and competitive spirit, Jordan revolutionized the game of basketball and transcended the sport to become a global icon. With six NBA championships, five Most Valuable Player awards, and numerous scoring titles, Jordan's impact on basketball and popular culture during the 1980s and beyond is immeasurable.

Question: What major sporting event did the Soviet Union boycott in 1984?

Answer: The Summer Olympics in Los Angeles

Trivia Snapshot: The Soviet Union led a boycott of the 1984 Summer Olympics held in Los Angeles, California, in response to the United States-led boycott of the 1980 Summer Olympics in Moscow. The Soviet Union and several other Eastern Bloc countries cited concerns over the safety and politicization of the Games as reasons for their boycott. The absence of these powerhouse nations had a significant impact on the competition but did not diminish the achievements of the athletes who participated.

Question: Which famous boxer, known as 'The Hitman', won world titles in five different weight divisions in the 1980s?

Answer: Thomas Hearns

Trivia Snapshot: Thomas Hearns, nicknamed "The Hitman," was a boxing sensation in the 1980s, winning world titles in five different weight divisions during his illustrious career. Known for his devastating punching power and exceptional reach, Hearns became a dominant force in the sport, earning legendary status among boxing fans worldwide. His epic battles with other boxing greats, including Sugar Ray Leonard and Roberto Durán, are etched in the annals of boxing history as some of the most memorable moments in the sport.

Question: In 1980, which English football club began a dominant period, winning their first European Cup and six First Division titles during the decade?

Answer: Liverpool F.C.

Trivia Snapshot: Liverpool Football Club, under the management of Bob Paisley and later Joe Fagan, embarked on a golden era in the 1980s, winning their first European Cup in 1981 and six First Division titles during the decade. Led by iconic players such as Kenny Dalglish, Graeme Souness, and Ian Rush, Liverpool established themselves as the dominant force in English and European football. Their success on the domestic and international stage solidified their place in football history and endeared them to fans around the world.

As we turn the final page of "The Golden Years Adult Trivia Book," I find myself reflecting on the vibrant tapestry of memories and moments that have defined the decades from the 1950s to the 1980s. It has been an exhilarating journey through the Fabulous Fifties, the Swinging Sixties, the Disco Seventies, and the MTV Eighties, each era echoing with its unique melody of music, TV, movies, sports, and influential personalities.

Your journey down Memory Lane, revisiting the cultural highlights and answering trivia that brought these golden years to life, has hopefully been as delightful as it was enlightening. Whether you reminisced about the days gone by or discovered the treasures of these decades, your engagement and enthusiasm have been the driving force behind this nostalgic odyssey.

This book was a labor of love, crafted to rekindle fond memories and spark lively conversations. Your participation in this trivia adventure has added another layer of joy to its creation. I hope these pages have brought smiles, sparked curiosity, and connected you more deeply with the rich tapestry of our shared history.

Thank you

B N William

Printed in Great Britain
by Amazon